Part 1

Airbrushing Basics

Chapter 1

THE AIRBRUSH

Airbrushing nails has been around for quite a while. Initially the only place to find an airbrush would be a hobby or craft store. Today you will find systems that have been designed for doing nails available from your professional beauty and nail distributor. I encourage you to shop from your professional beauty and nail distributor, since they are more likely to understand your needs than the hobby store. Many beauty and nail distributors are offering hands-on educational seminars to become better acquainted with your airbrushing equipment.

Airbrushes work on the same principle. All airbrushes combine air and paint to form an atomized spray for painting. Airbrushes differ in the (1) type of trigger action, (2) location of air and paint mixing, (3) ease of use and maintenance. Each airbrush has a small cone-shaped **fluid nozzle**, also called a **tip**, that a tapered needle fits into. When the **needle** fits snugly in the fluid nozzle, no paint is released when the trigger is depressed. When the needle is drawn back, the airbrush begins to release paint. The further the needle is drawn back, the more paint that is

TYPES OF AIRBRUSHES

	Single-Action	Traditional Double-Action	New Technology Double-Action
SATA#1	Long slender body with needle adjusting screw at back.		
SATA#2	Small stubby airbrush with needle adjusting knob.		
DATA#1		Asian manufactured airbrush	
DATA#2		American manufactured airbrush with small waxed in nozzle.	
DATA#3		American manufactured with self-centering nozzle.	
NEWTA#1			American manufactured; also called the variable action airbrush.
NEWTA#2			American manufactured with multi-action roller.
NEWTA#3			Airbrush in development that will be interchangeable with other new technology models.

released. The control of the amount of paint released varies by different types of airbrushes.

There are many different makes of airbrushes available on the market today. You want to avoid airbrushes that are designed for volume paint application; they are not economical or practical choices for airbrushing nails. Airbrushes that have a siphon bottle hanging below the body of the airbrush will take too long to change colors and do not offer the features you will want as a airbrush nail artist.

You want to choose an airbrush that is designed for small quantities of paint, is **gravity-feed** (gravity pulls the paint into the airbrush) and mixes the paint with air inside the airbrush (**internal mix**). This type of airbrush usually has a **well** or **small color cup** for the paint to be placed in the airbrush. A well (also called a **reservoir**) is a hole in the top of the airbrush, where drops of paint may be placed. If the airbrush has a color cup, it may be located on top of the airbrush or it may be attached to the side of the gun for the paint. (Figure 1-1)

Even though we have narrowed the scope of airbrushes to choose from, there are still many differences available. I am sure you will recognize your airbrush or the ones you have been researching from the following descriptions. Each airbrush has a disassembled/parts drawing. This is a generic drawing; your airbrush may have some slight differences. It is best for future reference if you retain the manufacturer's airbrush diagram that comes with your airbrush when you purchase it. This diagram will outline the correct assembly of your airbrush and contain the order numbers for parts in case you lose or break something.

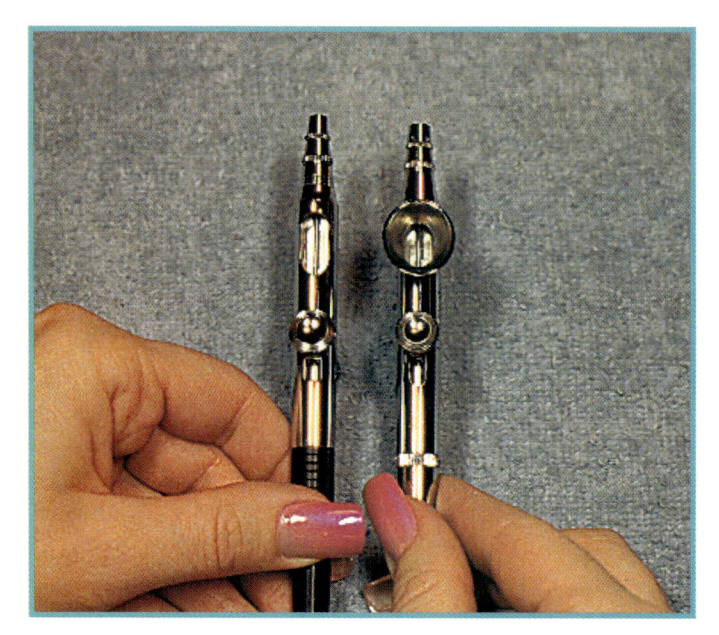

FIGURE 1-1: An airbrush with well (left), and an airbrush with color cup.

Types of Single-Action Airbrushes

A single-action airbrush releases air by depressing the trigger (the trigger may vary by manufacturer). The trigger has only one action that acts as an on and off switch for air. The paint spray is controlled by a needle adjusting screw or knob located somewhere else on the body of the airbrush. When the dial or knob is closed, the needle is seated snugly in the fluid nozzle and air escapes only when the trigger is depressed. When the **needle adjusting screw** or **knob** is turned, it begins to pull back the needle. The more you turn the screw or knob, the larger the opening in the nozzle and the more paint is released. There are two basic types of traditional single-action airbrushes we will consider:

1. **Long, slender body with a needle adjusting screw at the back.** (SATA#1) This type of airbrush has a well or color cup attached to the top of the airbrush. Air is released by depressing the trigger. Paint flow is adjusted by rotating the **needle adjusting screw** on the end of the airbrush. This adjustment requires a two-handed operation when adjusting the amount of paint to be released. (Figure 1-2a) The second screw from the end of the airbrush, the end screw, is the **needle chuck**. It is loosened only when the needle needs to be replaced. Refer to the airbrush diagram for location of parts in gun. (Figure 1-2b) This airbrush typically has interchangeable head assemblies and needles. For airbrushing nails, I find most people prefer a medium-head assembly used with a fine or medium needle. If you use a medium-head assembly with a fine needle, the needle will stick out further than usual. Be careful not to damage the delicate point of the needle. You may wish to pull the needle back into the airbrush body slightly when not in use or storing it. Some manufacturers wax the fluid nozzle into the head assembly. If this is the

FIGURE 1-2a: To adjust paint flow on this single-action traditional airbrush, rotate needle adjusting screw on the end of the airbrush.

1. Protective Cap	7. Trigger	13. Needler
2. Spray Regulator	8. Valve Casing	14. Needle
3. Head	9. "O" Ring	15. Needle Adjusting Screw
4. Teflon Head Washer	10. Plunger and "O" Ring	16. Needle Chuck
5. Teflon Needle Bearing	11. Plunger Spring	
6. Shell with Needle Bearing, no cup	12. Valve Screw	

FIGURE 1-2b: Diagram of single-action traditional airbrush #1 (SATA#1) and its parts. *(Courtesy of Ken Schlotfeldt, Badger Airbrush.)*

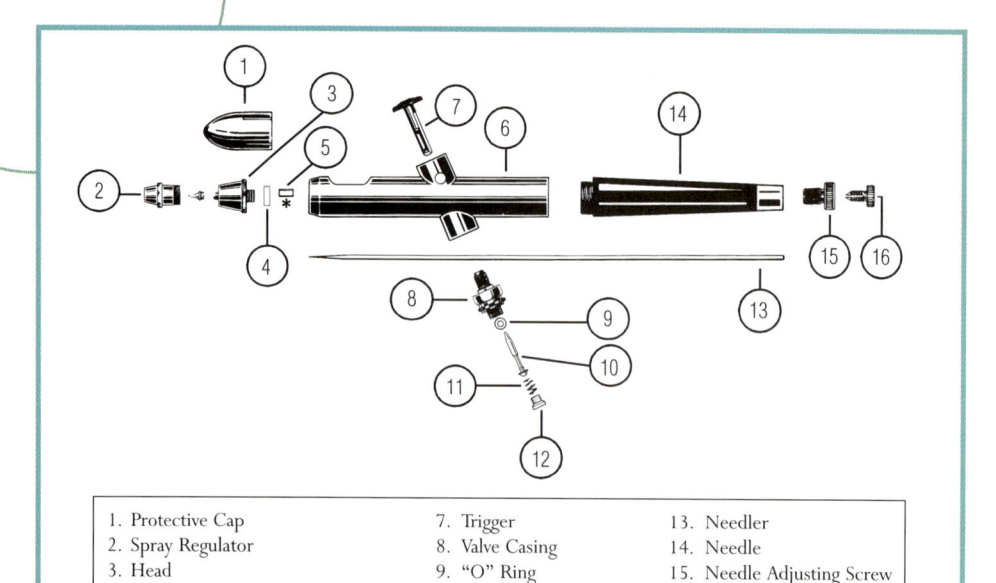

case, I recommend purchasing the pre-assembled head assembly. Other manufacturers have a system in which the fluid nozzle is held in place by the tightening of the head assembly over the nozzle, so the fluid nozzle alone may be replaced if damaged. I recommend that you have a spare needle and head assembly or nozzle on hand for this type of airbrush for quick repairs. This type of airbrush is manufactured by a number of American manufacturers and the parts are easily available.

2. **Small, stubby airbrush with needle adjusting knob.** (SATA#2) This airbrush comes with a color cup that attaches to

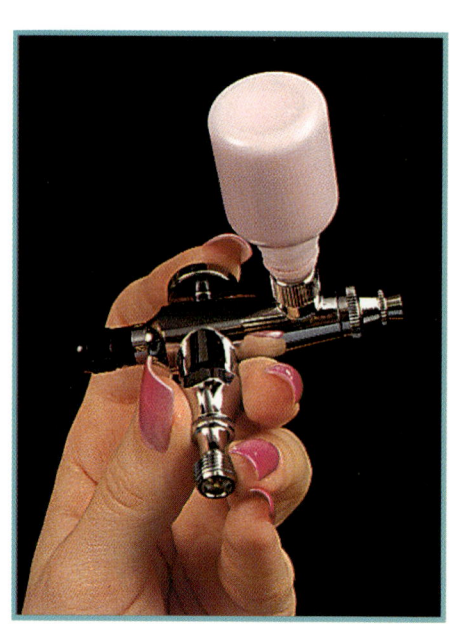

FIGURE 1-3: Stubby, single-action airbrush with paint bottle attached.

6   *Milady's Airbrushing for Nails*

the side; the cup is very large and I don't recommend using it for airbrushing nails. The opening for the color cup is large enough to hold adequate amounts of paint to airbrush nails. There is also an adapter available for this airbrush to hold a small paint bottle. (Figure 1-3) This bottle adapter permits quick color changes and no need to add paint while spraying, since it's unlikely you will run out of paint. This airbrush has a larger fluid nozzle than most

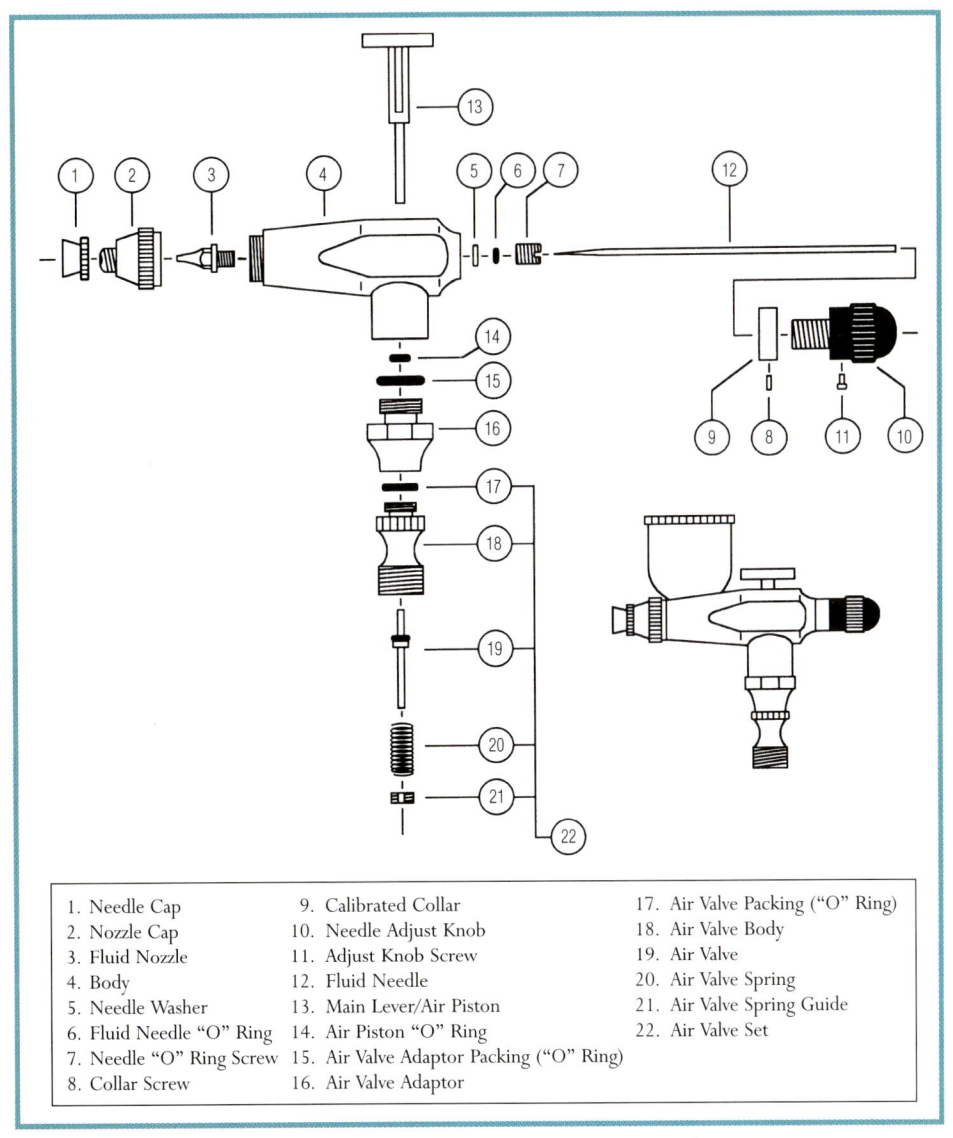

1. Needle Cap
2. Nozzle Cap
3. Fluid Nozzle
4. Body
5. Needle Washer
6. Fluid Needle "O" Ring
7. Needle "O" Ring Screw
8. Collar Screw
9. Calibrated Collar
10. Needle Adjust Knob
11. Adjust Knob Screw
12. Fluid Needle
13. Main Lever/Air Piston
14. Air Piston "O" Ring
15. Air Valve Adaptor Packing ("O" Ring)
16. Air Valve Adaptor
17. Air Valve Packing ("O" Ring)
18. Air Valve Body
19. Air Valve
20. Air Valve Spring
21. Air Valve Spring Guide
22. Air Valve Set

FIGURE 1-4: Diagram of Asian-made stubby single-action airbrush #2 (SATA#2) and its parts.
(Courtesy of Robert Tsunenaga, Olympos Airbrush, Professional Source, Inc.)

Airbrushing Basics

airbrushes, which reduces clogging. This airbrush is small enough to permit one-handed operation of both the trigger and needle adjusting knob. Depress trigger for air, turn knob to desired amount of opening to release paint. Refer to the airbrush diagram for location of parts in gun. (Figure 1-4) At this time there is only one size of nozzle and needle available. Remember to keep an extra of each on hand for quick repairs. This airbrush is manufactured in Japan. There is limited distribution of this gun, so parts may be a bit more difficult to locate (check with the distributor you purchased the airbrush from). The parts on this airbrush tend to be a bit pricey, depending on the exchange of the Japanese yen.

Types of Traditional Double-Action Airbrushes

The double-action airbrush trigger performs two functions, hence the name "double-action airbrush." The trigger operates both the release of air and controls paint flow. The trigger is depressed for air, and the paint flow is controlled by the distance the trigger is pulled back. Most **dual-action airbrushes** (Figure 1-5) release air when the trigger is pushed down; the paint is released when the trigger is drawn

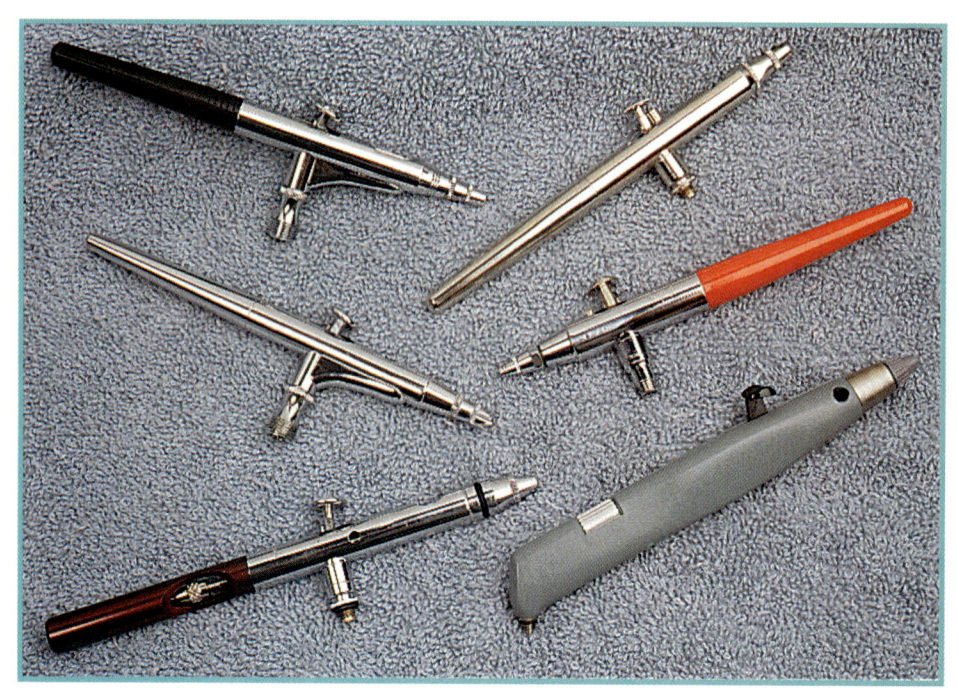

FIGURE 1-5: Dual action airbrushes.

back. The more the trigger is pulled back, the more paint that is released. You must be sure to pull back on the trigger while still depressing the trigger. If you pull back on the trigger, without pressing down the trigger first, you will release larger droplets of paint which will have a textured look rather than the desired smooth mist of color. The air must be released simultaneously with the paint to have a fine, atomized mist of paint. There are three types of **traditional double-action airbrushes** and two types of double-action airbrushes that use **new technology** that we will consider:

1. **Asian-manufactured double-action airbrush.** (DATA#1) This type of airbrush is manufactured by a number of Japanese companies, as well as private-labeled from Japan by a few American companies. It is a top quality (top price) professional graphic design airbrush, sold for fine to medium detail work. This airbrush is available with a color well or color cup on top of the airbrush, or with a color cup that attaches to the side. This airbrush is sold standard with a .2m fluid nozzle and needle. A .3m fluid nozzle is also available. I would recommend using your .2m needle with the larger .3m fluid nozzle if you are having clogging problems. One manufacturer is selling this model as a "nail airbrush" and fitting it with a .3m fluid nozzle, fluid needle and head assembly to reduce clogging. The fluid nozzle is extremely delicate and I recommend you exercise caution when cleaning it. (More on that later.) If you use the larger nozzle, your needle will stick out more than usual, so exercise care when storing the airbrush. You may wish to pull the needle back into the airbrush body slightly when not in use. The airbrush operates by pressing down on the trigger to release air. While pressing down for air, slowly draw back the trigger to release paint. As usual, I recommend keeping an extra needle and fluid nozzle on hand for repairs. Parts should be readily available for this type of airbrush. They tend to be a bit more pricey due to the cost of importing them from Asia. Refer to the airbrush diagram for location of parts in gun. (Figure 1-6)

2. **American-manufactured double-action airbrush with small, waxed-in nozzle.** (DATA#2) This airbrush is recommended by the manufacturer for precision work. It is usually sold with a fine, waxed-in fluid nozzle. There is a medium head assembly and needle available, which many people feel reduces clogging problems. The fluid nozzle is manufacturer-installed in the head assembly; when you need to replace this fluid nozzle, I recommend replacing the complete head assembly. You may use the fine needle or the medium needle with the medium head assembly. If you use the fine needle with the medium head assembly, the needle will stick out further than usual. You may wish to pull the needle into the airbrush body slightly when the airbrush is not in use. The recent models of this airbrush have two new features:

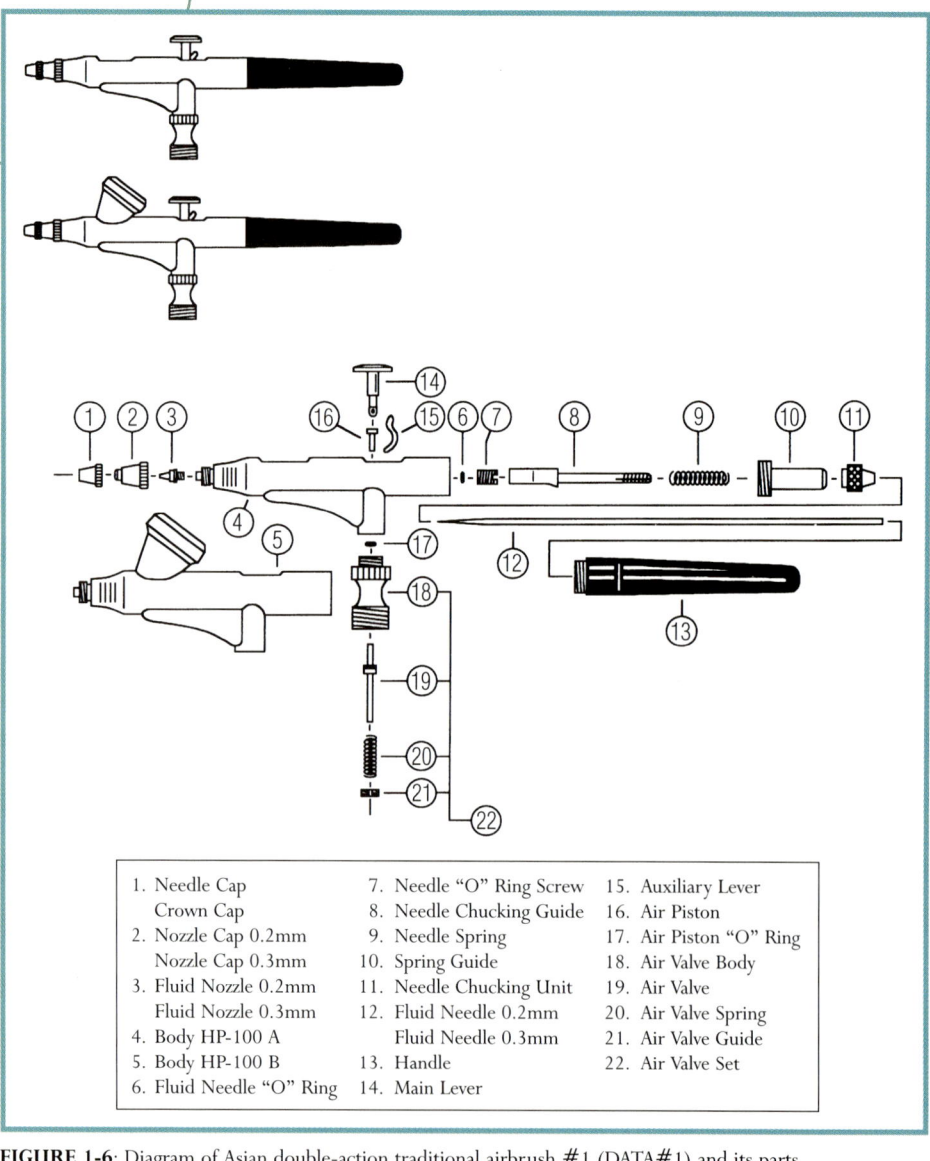

1. Needle Cap	7. Needle "O" Ring Screw	15. Auxiliary Lever
Crown Cap	8. Needle Chucking Guide	16. Air Piston
2. Nozzle Cap 0.2mm	9. Needle Spring	17. Air Piston "O" Ring
Nozzle Cap 0.3mm	10. Spring Guide	18. Air Valve Body
3. Fluid Nozzle 0.2mm	11. Needle Chucking Unit	19. Air Valve
Fluid Nozzle 0.3mm	12. Fluid Needle 0.2mm	20. Air Valve Spring
4. Body HP-100 A	Fluid Needle 0.3mm	21. Air Valve Guide
5. Body HP-100 B	13. Handle	22. Air Valve Set
6. Fluid Needle "O" Ring	14. Main Lever	

FIGURE 1-6: Diagram of Asian double-action traditional airbrush #1 (DATA#1) and its parts. *(Courtesy of Robert Tsunenaga, Olympos Airbrush, Professional Source, Inc.)*

A winged-back lever design for easy reassembly if the trigger comes out and an adjusting screw placed in front of the trigger. The adjusting screw may be rotated so it pushes the trigger back. This presets the trigger so every time you push down on the trigger, you will spray paint, similar to a single-action airbrush. The airbrush operates by pressing down on the trigger to release air.

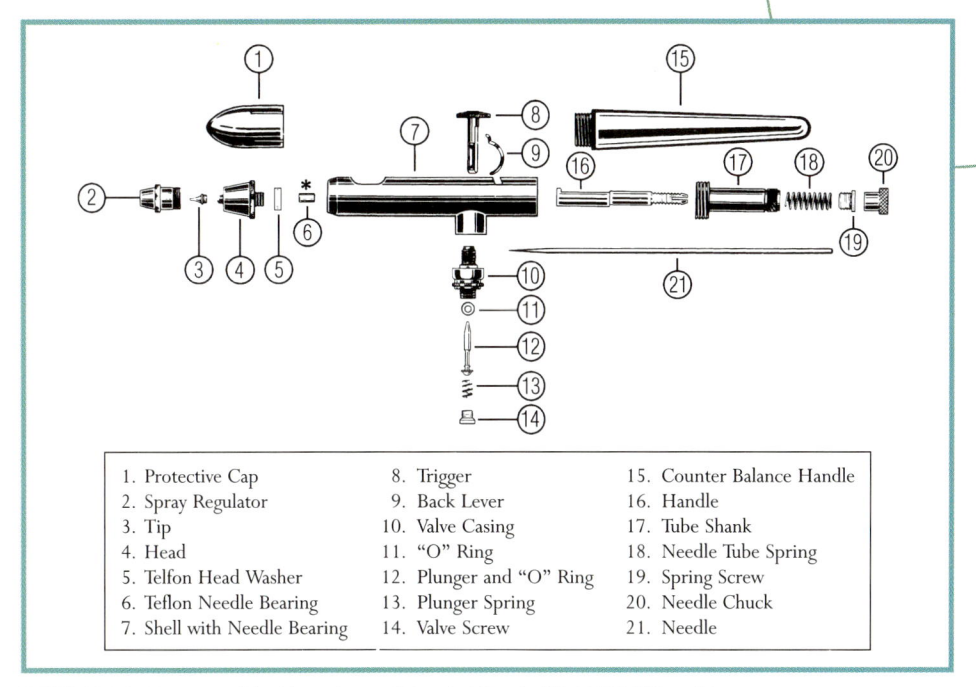

FIGURE 1-7: Diagram of double-action traditional airbrush #2 (DATA#2) and its parts. *(Courtesy of Ken Schlotfeldt, Badger Airbrush.)*

1. Protective Cap
2. Spray Regulator
3. Tip
4. Head
5. Teflon Head Washer
6. Teflon Needle Bearing
7. Shell with Needle Bearing
8. Trigger
9. Back Lever
10. Valve Casing
11. "O" Ring
12. Plunger and "O" Ring
13. Plunger Spring
14. Valve Screw
15. Counter Balance Handle
16. Handle
17. Tube Shank
18. Needle Tube Spring
19. Spring Screw
20. Needle Chuck
21. Needle

While pressing down for air, slowly draw back the trigger to release paint. I recommend keeping an extra needle and head assembly on hand for repairs. Parts should be readily available for this. type of airbrush. Refer to the airbrush diagram for location of parts in gun. (Figure 1-7)

3. **American-manufactured double-action airbrush with self-centering nozzle.** (DATA#3) This type of airbrush is sold with a fine, self-centering fluid nozzle. Even though the manufacturers call this nozzle a "fine" fluid nozzle, it is much larger than the fluid nozzles in DATA#1 and DATA#2. This fluid nozzle and needle size seems to perform well for airbrushing nails. One manufacturer makes this airbrush with a cut-away handle. This special handle permits direct access to the needle. If the airbrush clogs, you may pull directly on the needle chuck and blow out the clog. The airbrush operates by pressing down on the trigger to release air. While pressing down for air, slowly draw back the trigger to release paint. Parts should be readily available for this type of airbrush. Refer to the airbrush diagram for location of parts in gun. (Figure 1-8) You should have a spare needle and fluid nozzle on hand for repairs.

Airbrushing Basics 11

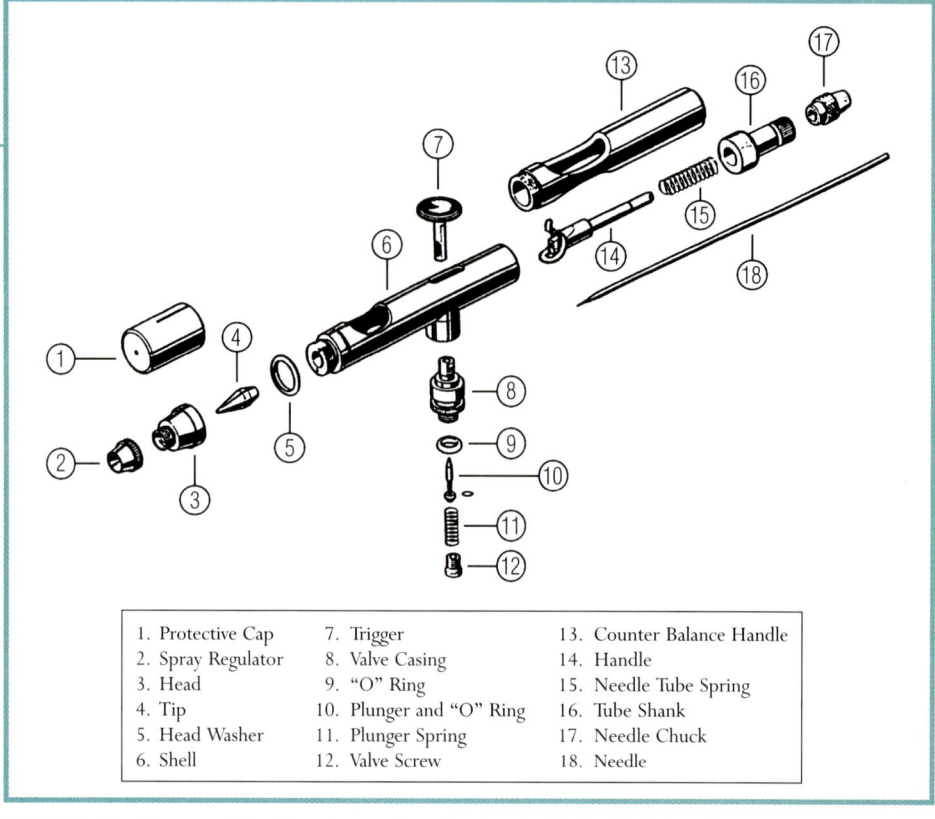

1. Protective Cap	7. Trigger	13. Counter Balance Handle
2. Spray Regulator	8. Valve Casing	14. Handle
3. Head	9. "O" Ring	15. Needle Tube Spring
4. Tip	10. Plunger and "O" Ring	16. Tube Shank
5. Head Washer	11. Plunger Spring	17. Needle Chuck
6. Shell	12. Valve Screw	18. Needle

FIGURE 1-8: Diagram of double-action traditional airbrush #3 (DATA#3) and its parts. *(Courtesy of Cal Petersen, Thayer & Chandler.)*

Types of New Technology Double-Action Airbrushes

1. **American-manufactured NEW TECHNOLOGY double-action airbrush.** (NEWTA#1) This variable-action airbrush uses patented technology to offer simple and unique features to the nail technician. There are only three parts to the airbrush that the user must be concerned with: the airbrush body, the nozzle and the color cup (or paint bottle) (Figure 1-9). The airbrush body never requires disassembly. The fluid nozzle contains a patented mechanism where the fluid nozzle and the needle are preset at the factory. The nozzle need never be disassembled. If you take the nozzle apart, you will not be able to reestablish the factory setting and the nozzle may not function properly.

   Before assembly, be sure the **actuator** or **adjuster lever** at the rear underside of the airbrush is set to the "+" side. This assures that the plunger pin inside the airbrush is retracted, out of the way for the nozzle. The airbrush is assembled by threading the gray nozzle finger-tight into the front of

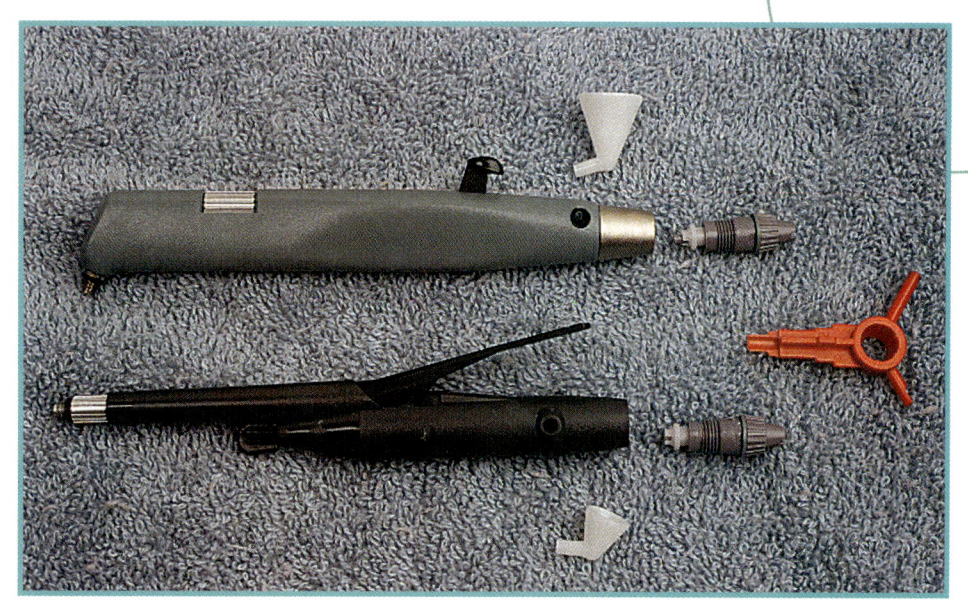

FIGURE 1-9: New Technology double-action airbrushes (NEWTA) and their parts. NEWTA#1 is black; NEWTA#2 is gray. *(Courtesy of James Mossop, Aztek Airbrush, Testor Corporation.)*

the airbrush. You may use the red tool, which is included, to tighten the nozzle a quarter turn into the airbrush. There should be a space between the airbrush and the nozzle. The general rule is if you are right-handed, place a blanking plug (small black plug) in the hole on the right side of the airbrush. (The plug is merely pushed in place by hand; there will be a slight gap between the edge of the plug and the airbrush.) Your color cup or paint bottle will attach on the left-side. If you are left-handed, your blanking plug is placed in the left hole and your color cup or paint bottle will attach on the right side. I recommend trying your air color cup on the right one time and the left the next. Whichever feels the most comfortable is correct for you.

The airbrush operates by pressing down on the lever to release air. Then press further down on the lever to release paint. You can control the amount of paint released by moving the actuator. I recommend starting with the actuator placed halfway between the "+" and "−" sign on the airbrush body. (Move the actuator *after* you have installed the nozzle.) You may increase the amount of paint released when the lever is pressed down by moving the actuator towards the "+". You will decrease the amount of paint released by moving the actuator towards the "−". This airbrush is constructed from a solvent-resistant resin which makes the airbrush very lightweight and durable. I recommend having a spare gray nozzle available. If the airbrush clogs, simply remove the nozzle and soak in cleaner. Put your spare nozzle in and you may resume spraying. These nozzles rarely break, but they may wear

Airbrushing Basics   *13*

out after six months or so. Have a few extra for replacement. Parts are readily available for this airbrush.

2. **American-manufactured New Technology double-action airbrush, with multi-action roller.** (NEWTA#1) This airbrush uses patented technology to offer simple and unique features to the nail technician. There are only three parts to the airbrush that the user must be concerned with: the airbrush body, the nozzle and the color cup (or paint bottle) (See Figure 1-7, gray airbrush at top of photo). There is a paint bottle adapter that permits direct insertion of the bottle instead of using a color cup; this bottle and all parts are interchangeable with NEWTA#1.

The airbrush body never requires disassembly. The airbrush is warrantied for life, as long as the body has not been tampered with or dismantled. The fluid nozzle contains a patented mechanism where the fluid nozzle and the needle are preset at the factory. The nozzle need never be disassembled. If you take the nozzle apart, you will not be able to reestablish the factory setting and the nozzle may not function properly.

The airbrush is assembled by threading the gray nozzle finger-tight into the front of the airbrush. You may use the red tool to tighten the nozzle a quarter turn into the airbrush. There should be a space between the airbrush and the nozzle. The general rule is if you are right-handed, place a **blanking plug** (small black plug) in the hole on the right side of the airbrush. Your color cup or paint bottle will attach on the left-side. If you are left-handed, your blanking plug is placed in the left hole and your color cup or paint bottle will attach on the right side. I recommend trying your air color cup on the right one time and the left the next. Whichever feels the most comfortable is correct for you.

The airbrush operates by pressing down on the trigger to release air. While pressing down for air, slowly draw back the trigger to release paint. This airbrush has a silver roller towards the top rear of the airbrush. This roller adjusts the position of the trigger. Roll the roller with your finger and watch the position of the roller change. When holding the airbrush, if you adjust the roller to your right, depress the trigger and pull back, more paint is released and the paint comes in quickly. If the roller is adjusted to your left, when you depress the trigger and start to pull back, first only air is released, then paint. More paint is released the further you pull back on the trigger. I find most nail technicians are comfortable with first turning the roller all the way to the left and then turning the roller a half turn or so back to the right. This sets the trigger to release air, then release small quantities of paint. If you desire more paint, pull back more or adjust the roller a bit more to the right.

This airbrush is constructed from a solvent-resistant resin which makes the airbrush very lightweight and durable. I recommend having a spare gray nozzle available. If the airbrush clogs, simply remove the nozzle and soak in cleaner. Put your spare nozzle in and you may resume spraying. There is a pink spatter nozzle that may be used for special effects in your nail art, like creating a snowy background or granite look. These nozzles rarely break, though they may wear out after six months or so. Have a few extra for replacement. Parts are readily available for this airbrush.

3. **An airbrush designed specifically for nail technicians** (NEWTA#3) **using the new technologies described in NEWTA#1 and NEWTA#2.** The nozzles, color cups and paint bottle adapters described in NEWTA#1 and NEWTA#2 will be interchangeable with the new nail airbrush. The nail airbrush is ergonomically correct and co-designed specifically for nail technicians by a nail technician. It will be available by the time this book goes to print. Please check with your professional beauty and nail distributor for more information.

Maintenance and Cleaning Procedures for Single-Action and Traditional Double-Action Airbrushes

The traditional, metal airbrush has many delicate parts which must be kept clean and lubricated for optimum performance. The maintenance and cleaning of traditional metal airbrushes, like SATA#1, SATA#2, DATA#1, DATA#2 and DATA#3, is very similar. Before operating your traditional airbrush for the first time you should become familiar with how to assemble, clean and maintain its components to prevent accidental damage to the airbrush. Once you begin airbrushing, it is critical that good cleaning habits are developed. If your airbrush is not cleaned and maintained properly, it will impair the performance of the airbrush.

Become familiar with the parts of your airbrush by studying the literature that accompanied the traditional airbrush when you purchased it. If you purchased or were given used equipment, contact the manufacturer. Most companies will be happy to provide you with the correct manufacturer's guidelines for maintenance of your equipment.

The following cleaning guidelines start with the first type of cleaning procedure, the **Paint Color Change**, which is the first step of any traditional airbrush cleaning procedure, and ends with your **Traditional Airbrush Weekly Maintenance**. I have found that it is best to spray some of your airbrush cleaner through your airbrush prior to adding paint. It lubricates the airbrush so paint flows through the airbrush easier.

CLEANING SUPPLIES

You will require some basic cleaning and maintenance supplies for your traditional metal airbrush.

- Paintbrush for cleaning color cup or reservoir.

CLEANING SUPPLIES

Single-Action or Traditional Double-Action Airbrushes	New Technology Airbrushes
Paintbrush for cleaning color cup or reservoir	Airbrush cleaner, dispensed in plastic squirt bottle
Real pipe cleaner	Red tool in airbrush kit
Airbrush cleaner, dispensed in plastic squirt bottle	Paintbrush for cleaning color cup and front of nozzle
Pure acetone	Terry and paper toweling
Grease or lubricant; no runny oils	Cleaning station, empty jar or rags
6" adjustable wrench	Small jar for soaking nozzles and color cup
Terry and paper toweling	
Cleaning station, empty jar or rags	

- Real pipe cleaners, the kind you find in the tobacco section of your drugstore (craft pipe cleaners will not work). Run the pipe cleaner through your fingers a few times prior to use to remove any lint.
- Airbrush cleaner recommended for use with your brand of paint. A plastic squirt bottle is the best type of dispensing container.
- Pure acetone for deep cleaning. NEVER SPRAY ACETONE THROUGH THE AIRBRUSH! I dip a pipe cleaner in acetone to rub away stubborn paint deposits.
- Grease or lubricant, available in hardware store or from airbrush manufacturer. The lubricant should be the consistency of petroleum jelly, no runny oils.
- A 6" adjustable wrench for assembling/disassembling airbrush. Most airbrushes come with a mini-wrench in the box. The 6" adjustable provides more control and ease.
- Terry and paper toweling
- Cleaning station, empty jar or rags to spray into.

STEP A: THE PAINT COLOR CHANGE

1. When you are finished with a paint color, spray the remaining color out of the airbrush into a jar, rag or cleaning station (Figure 1-10). Squirt your airbrush cleaner into the color cup or reservoir of the airbrush (Figure 1-11). Use your paintbrush and swirl away the paint residue (Figure 1-12). Spray the cleaner and paint out of your airbrush into your cleaning station. You may have to repeat this procedure for dark and pearlescent paints. Periodically, you should use your paintbrush to clean the front of the airbrush needle cap to carefully remove accumulated paint on the needle and needle cap.

FIGURE 1-10: A jar for use as cleaning station. This jar is fitted with a filter cap to trap paint. It reduces overspray.

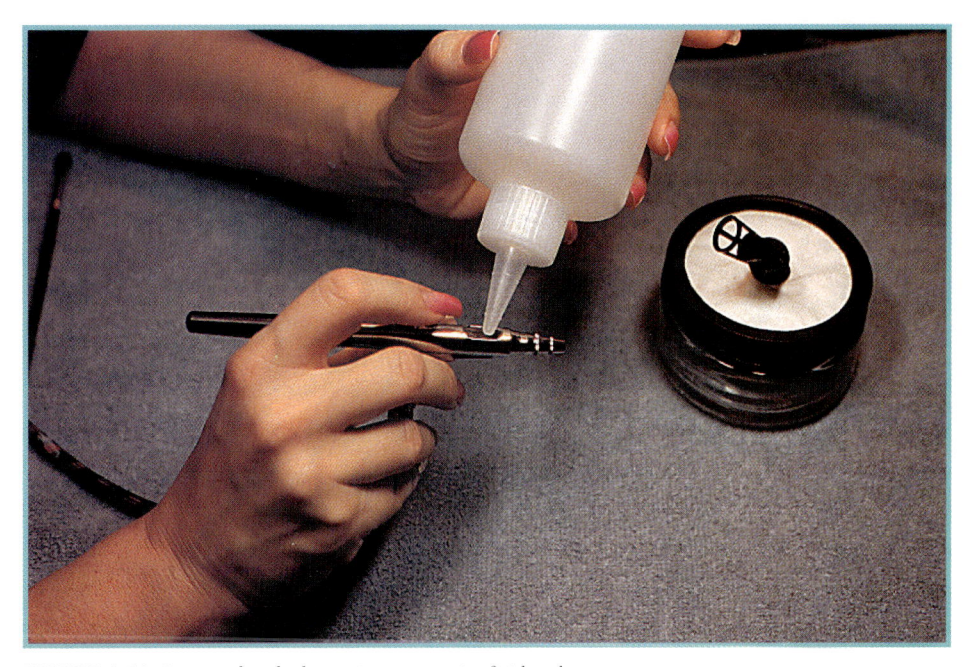

FIGURE 1-11: Squirt airbrush cleaner into reservoir of airbrush.

Airbrushing Basics 17

FIGURE 1-12: Use paintbrush to swirl away paint residue.

2. Add your next color and repeat step #1 when changing the paint colors. In some airbrushes, especially the New Technology Airbrushes, you will find a little color remaining in the spray after cleaning. Just move on to your next color and feed the new color through. Spray on table towel or in cleaning station until you see the new paint color.

STEP B: AFTER THE SERVICE IS COMPLETE

1. Airbrush your client's nails. Follow STEP A to clean your airbrush between paint colors. When finished, follow STEP A #1. Repeat STEP A #1 until the airbrush sprays no more color, just airbrush cleaner.
2. Remove handle (if your model has one). Carefully remove the needle from the airbrush and wipe clean. On your traditional dual-action airbrushes (DATA#1, DATA#2, DATA#3) merely loosen the needle chuck to remove the needle. If you remove it, you may lose it! NEVER PLACE ANY LIQUIDS IN AIRBRUSH WHEN THE NEEDLE IS REMOVED! The needle passes through a seal (o-ring) in the airbrush body and keeps liquids out of the back of the airbrush. Check the needle for snags by pinching the needle between your thumb and index finger, pull the needle through your finger and thumb. If you feel the needle snag your skin, go to the Troubleshooting Guide for more information. Replace the airbrush needle. In dual-action airbrushes, be careful to place the airbrush securely. While the needle is removed from

18   Milady's Airbrushing for Nails

double-action airbrushes, the trigger easily falls out. In some models, it is time consuming to replace. If the trigger falls out, see your manufacturer's directions for reassembly.
3. Wipe any dribbled paint from the sides of the reservoir or color cup.
4. Store airbrush until needed for next client.

STEP C: PERIODIC MAINTENANCE

Periodically, you should lubricate the trigger and o-ring located in the center of the body of the airbrush. You will know when the trigger requires lubrication; it will stick in the down position after you have released it with your finger. The needle passes through the o-ring and creates a seal to prevent paint or other liquids from going into the back of the brush or down the air valve. This o-ring becomes dried out from contact with airbrush cleaners and paint. When re-assembling airbrush at end of day for storage, place a small amount of lubricant (grease, not liquid oil) on base of trigger (prior to re-insertion of needle). Push trigger up and down a few times to work lubricant in. Dip needle into lubricant, (only a small amount is necessary) and re-insert needle through airbrush. Pull needle in and out of airbrush a few times to work lubricant in. (Figure 1-13) More lubricant may be applied to needle if airbrush has been neglected and o-ring still feels stiff (difficult to put needle through it.) I recommend spraying some water through airbrush after lubrication to remove excess lubricant that may have gone into the fluid nozzle.

When cleaning the traditional metal airbrushes, I never take them apart more than I described in the preceding directions. I am aware that other educators and manufacturers show people to take their airbrushes completely apart when cleaning them. Most airbrush nail artists have found my methods save time and avoid the loss of small parts that often occurs when the airbrush is totally disassembled. If you accidentally remove a part or lose your trigger from the gun, refer to the diagram that most closely resembles your airbrush in this book or look at your original directions to put your airbrush back together.

STEP D: END OF THE DAY CLEANING

Single-Action Airbrush (SATA#1 + SATA#2)

1. Follow STEP B, 1–3.
2. Remove the head assembly. I recommend work-

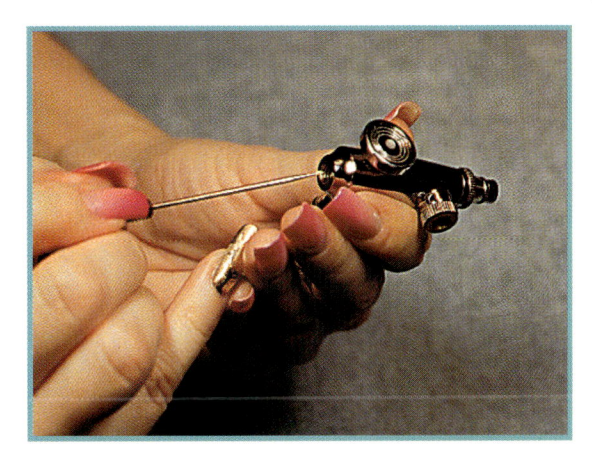

FIGURE 1-13: Pull needle in and out to work in lubricant.

ing over a towel to prevent losing any parts if they fall from the airbrush. The head assembly will separate into two parts. Bend the pipe cleaner in half to make a thicker cleaning surface for the needle caps.

SATA#1: To remove the head assembly, you will have to find the two flat surfaces on each side of the head assembly. Use the 6" adjustable wrench or the small wrench provided in your airbrush kit and turn the head assembly counter-clockwise to loosen. Remove the head assembly. Some models have a small plastic o-ring on the threaded male end. Be careful not to lose it. Separate the needle cap, sometimes called the spray regulator, and the nozzle cap. Use a pipe cleaner moistened with acetone to rub away paint accumulation. You may soak the fluid nozzle in most airbrush cleaners. If you have an airbrush model where the fluid nozzle is waxed into the head assembly, NEVER SOAK THIS PIECE IN ACETONE. I find soaking only necessary in very small nozzles that have not been cleaned regularly. Most times it will be adequate to use the pipe cleaner moistened with acetone to clean the back inside of the nozzle followed by scraping the inside of the fluid nozzle with a reamer made for your fluid nozzle or use an old needle.

SATA#2: To remove the head assembly, rotate the nozzle cap counter-clockwise. The head assembly consists of the nozzle and needle caps. Be careful to place the disassembled airbrush securely to avoid damage to the fluid nozzle. Separate the nozzle and needle caps. Use a pipe cleaner moistened in acetone to rub away accumulated paint. (Figure 1-14) At least once a week, more often if you are experiencing clogging, use the small wrench provided to remove the fluid nozzle. You may soak the fluid nozzle in airbrush cleaner or acetone for a few minutes to loosen up accumulated paint. Use a pipe cleaner to clean inside the back of the fluid nozzle. Use an old needle, reamer or small brush to clean the inside front of the fluid nozzle. Hold nozzle up to the light and make sure you can see through it.

3. Reassemble head assembly. If head assembly was difficult to take apart, place a dot of lubricant on threads before reassembling. This will make it easier to take apart next time. Check for o-ring on SATA#1.
4. Place head assembly back on airbrush body. If the trigger fell out, simply replace it back in the airbrush body.
5. If the fluid nozzle was removed from the airbrush body, you must loosen needle from locknut prior to re-inserting!

SATA#1: The needle must be separated from the needle adjusting screw and needle chuck.

SATA#2: The needle must be removed from the black knob. With a small screwdriver loosen the screw in the black knob counter-clockwise and pull the needle from the knob (Figure 1-15).

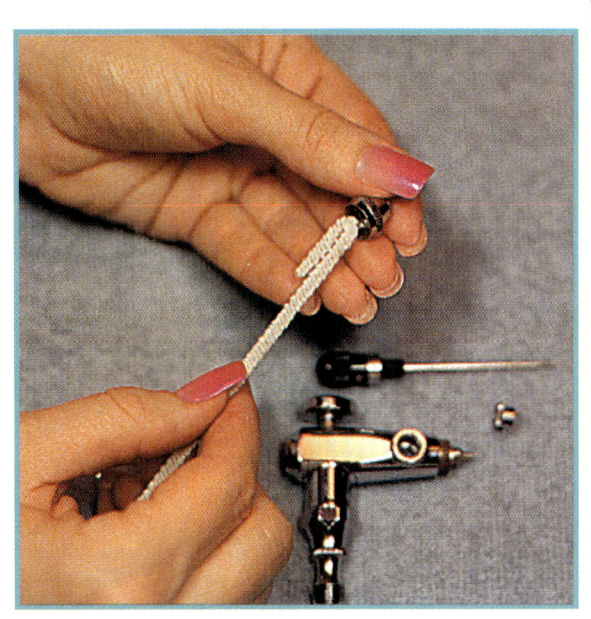

FIGURE 1-14: Use a pipe cleaner moistened in acetone to remove excess paint.

6. Check that the trigger is correctly lined up in airbrush body. It has a slot that the needle must pass through. Carefully replace needle. Push the needle as far forward as possible with your hand (NO TOOLS OR TAPPING ON TABLE. This may push the needle too far and through the fluid nozzle, cracking your nozzle.) When the needle is properly seated (as far forward in the nozzle as possible):

   - *SATA#1: Replace the needle adjusting screw and needle chuck. Tighten the screws into place.*
   - *SATA#2: Replace the black knob over the needle and thread down to the airbrush body. Use small screwdriver and tighten the screw in the black knob clockwise.*

7. Store airbrush carefully for next use.

Double-Action Airbrush (DATA#1, DATA#2, DATA#3)

1. Follow STEP B, 1–3.
2. Remove the head assembly. I recommend working over a towel to prevent losing any parts if they fall from the airbrush. To avoid the trigger falling out (it is time consuming to replace in most dual-action airbrushes) replace the needle in the airbrush. Withdraw the needle so it is not visible in the color cup or reservoir. The head assembly will separate into two parts. Bend the pipe cleaner in half to make a thicker cleaning surface for the needle caps. Tighten

Airbrushing Basics   *21*

FIGURE 1-15: Loosen and remove the screw in the black knob with a small screwdriver.

needle chuck to keep in place. If the color cup or reservoir needs more cleaning do not place any liquids in airbrush. Use a moistened pipe cleaner to rub accumulated paint away. Set airbrush aside and keep in a safe place.

> DATA#1: *Remove the head assembly by removing the nozzle and needle caps. Place the airbrush securely to avoid injuring the delicate fluid nozzle and having the trigger fall out. Separate the needle and nozzle caps. Use a pipe cleaner moistened in acetone to rub away accumulated paint. At least once a week, more often if you are experiencing clogging, use the small wrench provided to remove the fluid nozzle. Soak the fluid nozzle in airbrush cleaner or acetone for a few minutes to loosen up accumulated paint. Use an old needle, reamer or small brush to clean the inside of the fluid nozzle. Hold nozzle up to the light and make sure you can see through it.*

> DATA#2: *To remove the head assembly, you will have to find the two flat surfaces on each side of the head assembly. Use the 6" adjustable wrench or the small wrench provided in your airbrush kit and turn the head assembly counter-clockwise to loosen. Remove the head assembly. Some models have a small plastic o-ring on the threaded male end. Be careful not to lose it. Separate the needle cap, sometimes called the spray regulator, and the nozzle cap. Use a pipe cleaner moistened with acetone to rub away paint accumulation. You may soak the fluid nozzle in most airbrush cleaners. If you have an airbrush model where the fluid nozzle is waxed into the head assembly, NEVER SOAK THIS PIECE IN ACETONE. I find soaking only*

necessary in very small nozzles, that have not been cleaned regularly. Most times it will be adequate to use the pipe cleaner moistened with acetone to clean the back inside of the nozzle followed by scraping the inside front of the fluid nozzle with a reamer made for your fluid nozzle or use an old needle. Hold the fluid nozzle up to the light and make sure you can see through it.

DATA #3: To remove the head assembly, you will have to find the two flat surfaces on each side of the head assembly. Use the 6" adjustable wrench or the small wrench provided in your airbrush kit and turn the head assembly counter-clockwise to loosen. Remove the head assembly. I recommend holding the airbrush with the nozzle end up. When you remove the head assembly, the fluid nozzle must be removed since it is held in place by the head assembly. Separate the needle and nozzle cap. Use a pipe cleaner moistened with acetone to rub away paint accumulation. Since the fluid nozzle is unattached, you may wish to clean the inside of the nozzle with the pipe cleaner as well to prevent paint buildup. Use an old needle or reamer to scrape inside front of fluid nozzle. Hold fluid nozzle up to the light and make sure you can see through it.

3. Reassemble head assembly. If head assembly was difficult to take apart, place a dot of lubricant on threads before reassembling. This will make it easier to take apart next time.

4. Replace fluid nozzle if removed. Replace the head assembly. THE FRONT OF THE AIRBRUSH MUST ALWAYS BE ASSEMBLED PRIOR TO REPLACING AND SEATING THE NEEDLE!

Press down on trigger to make sure it is properly placed. If the trigger does not work, re-adjust it to the correct position. Carefully replace needle. Push the needle as far forward as possible with your fingers (NO TOOLS OR TAPPING ON TABLE. This may push the needle too far and through the fluid nozzle, cracking your nozzle). When the needle is properly seated (as far forward in the nozzle as possible) tighten the needle chuck. Replace the handle.

5. Store airbrush carefully for next use.

Maintenance and Cleaning Procedures for New Technology Airbrushes

The new technology airbrushes have significantly reduced the amount of time it takes to clean an airbrush. This new technology eliminates bent needles and cracked fluid nozzles of traditional airbrushes.

CLEANING SUPPLIES

The supplies you will require to clean and maintain the new technology airbrushes are:

- Airbrush cleaner recommend for use with your brand of paint. A plastic squirt bottle is the best type of dispensing container.
- The red tool provided in airbrush kit
- A paintbrush for cleaning in color cup and front of nozzle [a soft toothbrush works well for cleaning the front of the nozzle.]
- Terry and paper toweling
- Cleaning station, empty jar or rags to spray into.
- Small jar for soaking nozzles and color cup. (I have been using an empty film canister, since it is airtight and unbreakable.)

STEP A: THE PAINT COLOR CHANGE

1. When you are finished with a paint color, spray the remaining color out of the airbrush into a jar, rag or cleaning station. Squirt airbrush cleaner into the color cup or open orifice of the airbrush. Use your paintbrush to swirl away paint residue from color cup or orifice of airbrush. Spray cleaner and paint out of your airbrush into your cleaning station. You may have to repeat this procedure for dark and pearlescent paints. If you do not have the color cup attached, you may squirt cleaner directly into the airbrush while simultaneously pulling back on trigger and blowing out airbrush cleaner. (Called a "power cleaning"). Periodically, you should use your paintbrush to clean the front of the airbrush nozzle to remove accumulated paint on the needle and nozzle.

2. Add your next color and repeat step #1 when changing the paint colors. If only a little hint of color remains, add the next color and feed it through the airbrush. Spray on table towel or into cleaning station until you see the new paint color.

STEP B: AFTER THE SERVICE IS COMPLETE

1. Airbrush your client's nails. When finished, follow STEP A #1 to clean your airbrush between colors. Repeat STEP A #1 or simply remove the gray nozzle with the red tool provided in your kit, brush the front of it with your paintbrush (soft toothbrush works well on this airbrush) and place with the color cup in a small jar with airbrush cleaner. (Figure 1-16). When cleaning

FIGURE 1-16: Remove gray nozzle with red tool.

nozzles, do not disassemble. If you take the nozzle apart, you will not be able to reestablish the factory setting and the nozzle will not function properly.
2. Power clean the airbrush into a towel and put away until next client.
3. When next client arrives, shake storage jar, remove clean nozzle and color cup. Place nozzle and color cup into airbrush and you are ready to airbrush.

STEP C: END OF THE DAY CLEANING

The end of the day cleaning is the same as outlined above in STEP B. Periodically, insert the reamer end of the red tool into the front of the airbrush, where the nozzle is normally threaded in. Carefully push the reamer in. Watch that you do not injure the plunger pin located inside the airbrush body. Rotate the reamer 360° and remove. Push down on the trigger and blow out any paint lumps which have come free. Repeat procedure if necessary.

Air Sources and Hardware

Chapter 2

Air Hoses

The air hose connects the airbrush to the air source. Each airbrush has a unique size fitting; be sure that the size fitting on your hose will fit your airbrush. It is best if you buy them at the same time. The end of the hose which attaches to your **moisture separator** or **air compressor** is usually a 1/4" thread; although, there are a few compressor manufacturers who have a different size fitting. If you have a hose that does not attach to one or both pieces of equipment, adapters are available.

There are three basic types of airbrush hose available. There are **straight plastic hoses** which come in a variety of colors and quality of plastic. The second type of hose commonly used is a **coiled plastic hose** which stretches when in use and re-coils when not. This prevents your hose from laying on the floor. It is also available in different colors and quality of plastic. The third type of hose is a rubber hose with a braided fabric cover. **Braided rubber hose** is a durable hose recommended for use with traditional metal airbrushes. If you have chosen one of the new lightweight, resin airbrushes, use the hose provided in the airbrush kit. Braided hose will be heavier than the resin airbrush and feel unbalanced.

Airbrush hose is available in assorted lengths. Most companies sell a length of 6 to 10 feet as a standard size. You will usually be close enough to your air source that this should be adequate. If you are setting up a large salon and want to use a large air source located in a rear closet and send air hose to each airbrush station, I recommend contacting the manufacturer of your air hose. They will be able to custom cut the air hose and provide the supplies for your needs. If you are going to run air hose to each set-up, you will want to place the air hose inside a dropped ceiling or a pipe system commonly used in offices for phone wires. This will conceal the air hose for safety and preserve the appearance of the salon.

Air Sources

Today there is quite a selection of air sources for the airbrush artist. The air source is a vital piece of equipment since it provides the pressurized or compressed air that atomizes the airbrush paint and provides the mist of color for our nail designs. The

AIR SOURCES

	Propellant Air Canister	Compressed Air Tank	Diaphragm or Small Piston Compressor	Storage and Silent Compressor
Cost	Inexpensive to start.	Inexpensive, but usually requires deposit or purchase of compressed gas cylinder.	$100 to $300	$400 and up
Advantages	Portable. Good for beginners.	Good when used when electricity is not available; quiet and moistureless.	Portable, no maintenance, and long life spans. Unlimited supply of compressed air.	Unlimited supply of compressed air; quiet; can operate with more than one airbrush.
Disadvantages	Expensive in long run. Runs out of air halfway to two-thirds of the way through the can.	Must have spare tank on hand.	Makes noise.	Requires maintenance.

pressure of the air being fed into your airbrush hose is measured by **pounds per square inch (psi)**. I prefer to work around 30–35psi when airbrushing nails; however, I know some people prefer to work at lower (20–25psi) and higher (35–40psi) pressures. I recommend experimenting with your equipment to find the best pressure for your equipment and brand of paint.

PROPELLANT AIR CANISTER

The airbrush propellant may be the first exposure the nail artist receives to an air source. Some manufacturers include a can in inexpensive kits to give the fledgling airbrush artist an immediate start at trying the airbrush. Propellant air canisters are manufactured by many different companies but basically operate under the same principles. Some **propellant can adapter/valves** act as a regulator which permit you to control how much air is released into your air hose, while others just act as an "on and off" switch. The propellant should state the maximum pressure it will maintain if kept at a constant temperature (usually room temperature or 70° F).

1. Always keep the propellant can in upright position when connecting fittings and during use. Inversion of can during use may discharge liquid propellant which may cause frostbite upon skin contact. Do not shake can prior or during use.
2. The protective cap is removed from the propellant can and an adapter must be attached. There is a small pin inside the adapter which fits into the top of

Airbrushing Basics

the air canister. Be sure the pin is retracted into the adapter (closed), or else when you thread on the adapter, air will begin to escape. Screw the adapter on as far as possible. It will operate the self-sealing valve in the can. If you remove the adapter after use, the can will self-seal again and you will not lose any air.

3. After attaching the adapter, attach your airbrush hose (a propellant air canister adapter for the hose may be required) to the adapter. (Figure 2-1)

4. Connect your airbrush to the other end of the hose and you are ready to airbrush.

FIGURE 2-1: Compressed air tank with plastic washer between outlet and regulator.

If you experiment with propellant air canisters, you will find that halfway to two-thirds of the way through your can the pressure will drop. You might notice that the adapter valve actually "freezes up" from the air escaping through it. If you place the canister in a shallow pan of room-temperature water, this will help you get the most out of your air propellant canister.

Air propellant canisters are an inexpensive way to get a taste of airbrushing. They may be useful in situations where electricity is unavailable or not recommended (like a photo shoot). However, most people agree that in the long run, air propellant canisters are more expensive than investing in a diaphragm compressor and far more frustrating!

COMPRESSED AIR TANK

If you want an air source that is quiet and does not require electricity, a **compressed air tank** or **compressed gas cylinder** may be what you need. Compressed air is available from a local beverage supply company or a welding supply company (I am told the latter is a better source because their CO_2 tends to be drier and cleaner than the soda fountain gas). They will usually require you to purchase or place a deposit on the cylinder itself. I use a company that after my initial deposit was paid for my cylinders, they trade my empty cylinders for full ones and I pay for the air and delivery.

The most commonly used compressed air is carbon dioxide or CO_2. I use CO_2 tanks for seminars when operating 20 air compressors simultaneously would be prohibitive (not enough electrical power at the location). I use 20 lb. tanks since I can move them if necessary. The tanks are very heavy when full and must be placed securely. Anything larger than a 20 lb. tank is too heavy to move without a dolly. You will require an **air tank regulator** or **control valve** to control the release of air into your airbrush hoses. The regulator should have a **pressure gauge** to set the correct pressure (25–35psi) and maintain a constant pressure for airbrushing nails. Some regulators have a second gauge which tells you how much air is left in the tank. From my experience, you may use up to four airbrushes simultaneously from the tank (at 35 psi). This is accomplished by attaching multiple **manifolds** to the regulator to permit multiple hose attachments. (See the manifold section) If you use more than four airbrushes, you risk freezing up the regulator which will shut down the air flow. If this occurs, place a warm towel over the regulator to defrost it slowly. Reduce the number of airbrushes attached to the regulator. You may continue airbrushing when the regulator defrosts and the air flow resumes.

Large salons may wish to have a small closet at the rear of the nail area and run hoses from large compressed gas cylinders (50 lbs.) to each station. The compressed air is delivered moisture-free and silently. When the tank in use runs out, you must have a spare *full* tank in the closet to switch the regulator to. Call the supply service and have them replace the empty tank for a full one immediately, so you are prepared when the current compressed gas cylinder is empty.

1. When using a compressed air tank, one must be sure the tank is secured in an upright position. If the tank falls over and breaks the stem, the tank may explode or become a flying torpedo as the compressed air is released. WHEN USING A COMPRESSED GAS CYLINDER EXERCISE EXTREME CAUTION! The compressed air tank must be used upright or you run the risk of liquid CO_2 coming down the air hose or spilling.

2. Most suppliers of compressed air tanks offer delivery and pickup of the compressed gas cylinders. The gas cylinders should be transported upright in an open truck. Transporting compressed gas cylinders in enclosed vehicles increases the risk of explosion in the case of leakage. If you must use a passenger vehicle to transport the cylinders, the trunk should be kept partially open for the entire period cylinders are in it.

3. Place Teflon tape (plumber's tape found in hardware store) clockwise around the tank outlet. A plastic disc or washer (sold with regulator) is placed between the tank outlet and the tank regulator. (Figure 2-2) Thread the tank regulator onto the tank by hand. Tighten with an adjustable wrench until tight. Attach hoses and airbrushes to open outlets on the regulator. (Figure 2-3)

FIGURE 2-2: Compressed air tank with plastic washer between outlet and regulator.

FIGURE 2-3: Compressed air tank with hoses attached.

Milady's Airbrushing for Nails

4. Make sure regulator valve is in closed position. Open the tank valve at the top of stem on the compressed gas cylinder. You will hear a slight hiss as air escapes into the regulator. The air is now waiting at the regulator to be released into your air hoses. Air hoses and air brushes must be attached before next step.

5. Adjust regulator valve to release desired air pressure into your air hoses. You may need to release air from one of your airbrushes to set the pressure accurately. Some regulators have a handle to adjust this pressure; other units have a screw. This screw may be adjusted by hand or require a screwdriver or coin to turn.

Compressed air tanks cost very little to run and maintain. When electricity is hard to come by such as at an outdoor fair or when fluctuations in voltage will not be tolerated (like in a photo or TV studio), compressed air tanks are ideal. Many people use CO_2 tanks since it is moistureless and quiet in the salon.

When using compressed air tanks, one must remember that when you run out of air, you are out of air. You must have a spare tank to move the regulator to or another air source available like an air compressor. Compressed gas cylinders must be secured to a wall or in a closet (with an open top) to avoid toppling the tanks with a pull on an air hose. Compressed air tanks are an excellent air source as long as you understand their limitations and safety requirements.

AIR COMPRESSORS

Air compressors are by far the most popular air source for the airbrush artist. There is quite an array of makes, models and versions of the air compressor available. Let's look at the few types which suit our airbrush nail purposes. The obvious advantage of an air compressor is that as long as you have electricity, you have an unlimited supply of compressed air. I recommend the use of a moisture trap and pressure regulator with all compressors. I will discuss these necessary accessories following the compressor descriptions.

The Diaphragm or Small Piston Compressor is the smallest and most economical type of compressor available. (Figure 2-4) There are dozens of different brands available which fall into a price range of $100 to $300. As with anything, you usually get what you pay for. You must evaluate what your specific needs are and which compressor meets your requirements best. Key points to evaluate are as follows:

1. All diaphragm and small piston compressors will make a certain amount of noise. Some are very loud (usually lower cost) while others are no louder than a blow-dryer. What amount of noise will be acceptable for your working environment? I have found most nail technicians work in salons where the noise level equivalent to a blow-dryer is not noticeable. The best way to evaluate

FIGURE 2-4: Diaphragm compressor is portable and most economical compressor available.

how much noise a compressor will make is to plug it in with an airbrush hose and airbrush attached. (The compressor will sound louder when it is unattached to the airbrush and hose.) There are industrial diaphragm compressors which are very noisy and are not suitable for use in a salon environment.

2. How much air pressure does the compressor actually produce? Most companies will state the pressure their compressor produces when unattached to the airbrushes and hoses ("no load" on compressor). But the air pressure is usually 10 to 15 psi less than that number produced when the compressor is attached to equipment. You are going to want a compressor that will at least meet the 25 psi minimum air pressure when attached to your airbrush equipment (compressor is "under load"). Ideally, you will be able to adjust your pressure from 25 to 35 psi with a **compressor regulator** to determine your optimum air pressure for your equipment and paint when under load.

3. While you are spraying, the small compressor is running constantly. Some models are not designed to run longer than thirty minutes at a time; when they are in danger of over-heating there is a safety switch that automatically shuts the compressor off (called **automatic thermal protection**). The compressor will not start again until it has sufficiently cooled off. This is a dilemma when practicing or trying to complete nail designs that require more than 30 minutes of spraying time. There are models available that run constantly for eight hours a day. These units are manufactured to run for long periods and are better thermally protected to prevent the compressor from shutting off after a short time of spraying (the unit will shut off if something

is wrong and the unit is overheating). This would be a more desirable type of compressor since you will have adequate time to practice or complete intricate designs without worrying about running out of compressed air.

4. Investigate the type of warranty that is included with your compressor. Most companies have a 12-month warranty, while some have as little as 6 months and others have as much as 24 months. Before you buy, I recommend finding out who you should contact for service if you have mechanical problems.

5. Some compressors come with a feature called automatic shut-off. An automatic shut-off compressor does not operate unless the trigger on your airbrush is depressed. When you are not using the airbrush, the compressor shuts itself off. Some nail artists prefer this feature to reduce the compressor sound in the salon. I have found the automatic shut-off compressor a difficult compressor to work with. I find that when you release the trigger, the pressure builds in the compressor. When you first release the trigger, a gust of air is released followed by a lowering of pressure. If you continue to spray, the pressure levels off until you stop. Each time you spray this "pulsating" pressure occurs. I have found this irregularity to affect the performance of my airbrush and it seems to really frustrate new airbrush artists. If you have an automatic shut-off small compressor, you may open the body and change the settings to stop the automatic shut-off feature. Most compressors may be reset for automatic shut-off again if you decide it was a feature you preferred. Contact the manufacturer for instructions on how to do this on your compressor. I prefer to control my compressor with an "on and off" switch. Some models come with a switch on the compressor; others have foot pedals or power outlet strips with a button to turn the compressor on and off.

6. If you are going to travel often with your small compressor, weight may be another thing to consider. The compressors that fall into this category weigh between six and twelve pounds. Many nail techs like to bring their compressor home with them to practice their techniques in the privacy of their home and need to bring the compressor back the next day. As an educator, I travel with my equipment and the weight is definitely a factor. I have found a lightweight compressor without sacrificing performance.

To operate your small compressor, please start by reading the manufacturer's directions. You will save yourself time and money if you know how to operate your electrical equipment properly from the start. Check if you have an **external bleeder valve** which must be open prior to starting the compressor. After starting the compressor, close the bleeder valve down to a point where only a pin-hole of air is escaping to prevent a back-up of air pressure into the compressor. Each time you restart the compressor you may have to reopen the bleeder valve or depress the trigger of your airbrush to get the compressor to start. If your directions do not discuss an external bleeder valve, then you probably have a unit which has a built-in or internal bleeder valve. If you are unsure contact the manufacturer.

Most small compressors will vibrate and the compressor will become hot to the touch when in operation. Most units have automatic thermal protection which will shut off the compressor if overheated. To re-start, release air pressure and let the compressor cool down. Be sure to place the compressor on the floor. To prevent it from dancing across the floor, place a carpet remnant or one of the pads designed to muffle a typewriter or calculator (available at an office supply) on the floor. If it is an uncarpeted floor, I would recommend using a carpet tape to keep the compressor from dancing across the floor. Some of the compressors have black rubber feet that leave marks in the carpet after it has heated up during operation. A carpet or pad will prevent damage to your floor.

The small compressor is an excellent, economical choice for an endless supply of air as long as you have electricity. They are portable, require no maintenance, have long life spans, and are inexpensive. There are small compressors that will meet everyone's professional and financial needs. I have found that investing in the right equipment from the start may save you money in the long run; rather than having to replace existing equipment after finding out it does not meet your professional requirements.

The Storage and Silent Compressors are the larger compressors that many artists move up to after they have become proficient at airbrushing and are ready to make a larger financial commitment. (Figure 2-5). The cost of these compressors starts around $400 and goes up from there. Many of these compressors have storage tanks which fill to capacity, then shut-off until the storage tank level diminishes. These compressors tend to be much quieter than the smaller compressors; many produce a hum or blow-dryer sound when compressing air and filling the storage tank. The best way to determine noise level is to run the compressor with your airbrush and hose attached. Even compressors marketed as "silent" tend to hum when in operation.

FIGURE 2-5: Storage and Silent Compressor is larger and more expensive.

1. The larger compressors generally require a bit of maintenance. Most require oil and have an oil gauge that must be monitored regularly. Refer to the manufacturer's diagrams and instructions shipped with your compressor unit. New compressors are shipped without oil for safe transportation. Remove the protective cap on the oil spout and store in safe place. (If you send your compressor for service, you may need to empty the oil first.) Add approved type of oil to the level indicated by the glass oil gauge when the level is low. Put air intake filter in place over oil spout. Change the oil regularly per manufacturer's directions. There are some oil-less compressors; they generally use a fan (air) instead of oil to cool the motor.
2. Clean the air intake filter per manufacturer's directions. When transporting your compressor, remove air filter and replace with protective cap.
3. A layer of water will gradually build up in the storage tank. Be sure the storage tank is empty of air. Open the drain-tap to let the water out. You will need a towel to absorb the water as it comes out of the tank. Do this at least once a week to avoid rusting of the tank.
4. Inquire how often and where you will have to bring (ship?) the compressor for maintenance or repair services.

Large compressors have many advantages. They offer an unlimited supply of compressed air when electricity is available. They tend to be quieter than small compressors and are dependable with proper maintenance. Most larger compressors will operate more than one airbrush; some are strong enough to operate up to five and six airbrushes simultaneously. If you make the investment in a large compressor, you must make the commitment to the maintenance it requires.

Air Pressure Regulators

There are two types of **air pressure regulators**. The first type of air pressure regulator is the compressed air tank regulator. This type of regulator is discussed in detail under the compressed air tank section. (See page 28)

The second type of air pressure regulator is designed to attach to air compressors. A pressure regulator should be used on most compressors to set the air pressure desired to airbrush nails. Most nail technicians use an air pressure between 25 psi and 35 psi. Experiment using different air pressures until you find the pressure that works best for you and your equipment. Many times the air pressure regulator and the moisture separator are combined into one unit.

The air pressure regulator should be adjusted after the airbrush and air hoses have been attached to the compressor and the compressor has been turned on. Pull up on the **pressure adjusting knob** and adjust air pressure. Push down on the pressure adjusting knob to lock desired air pressure in place. Air pressure may be adjusted as needed. Do not turn pressure adjusting knob when locked in place; this action may cause damage to the knob assembly.

Moisture Separator

A compressor uses the air in the room you are working in. The air contains moisture and dirt which will affect the quality of your work. The moisture in the air will collect in your air hose and eventually will "spit" unto your work surface. This will cause your airbrush paint to smear, run or never dry correctly. After using the airbrush and compressor for a period of time (it doesn't take long, especially in high humidity) remove your airbrush from the air hose. The air hose should still be connected to the running compressor. The air hose will be blowing air. Put the air hose next to your hand and feel the water droplets shoot into your hand. A moisture separator (also called a **moisture trap**) will prevent this accumulation of water in the hose.

Most manufacturers recommend attaching the moisture separator directly to the outlet on the compressor. I have found that moisture still accumulates in my air hose and will spatter onto my work, especially when using a small compressor. The small compressor becomes hot while in operation. I have found that the air is so hot, that the vaporized moisture easily passes through the moisture separator and then will start **condensing** (water droplets cooling and collecting) in the cooler air hose.

To prevent this many airbrush experts recommend placing a five or six foot air plastic hose from the compressor to the moisture separator. When the hot air exits the compressor it will encounter the plastic hose and cool down. It will then enter the moisture separator. The moisture separator (and regulator, if a combined unit) must be mounted to the wall or your table in an upright position to operate correctly. (Industrial strength Velcro® works well.) The air hose or manifold containing the air hoses should be attached to the other side of the moisture trap. (Figure 2-6) Now the air will cool in the first air hose. When it reaches the moisture trap, the cooled water droplets and any debris will be caught successfully by the moisture trap. Only dry, clean air will pass into the air hoses leading to your airbrushes. The moisture separator ideally should be located somewhere between the height of the compressor (which is low, on the ground) and your work surface (which is high, at the top of a table). In the event that a bit of moisture should still escape the moisture separator, if the hose is traveling up to the airbrush, water droplets will tend to roll down and get caught in the moisture trap.

At the end of each day, loosen the drain valve (looks like a screw) or press up the pin located at the base of your moisture separator to drain the moisture from the bowl. Your compressor and airbrush should still be attached forcing the air with water droplets out through the drain valve. Follow your manufacturer's recommended directions for cleaning and maintenance of your moisture separator.

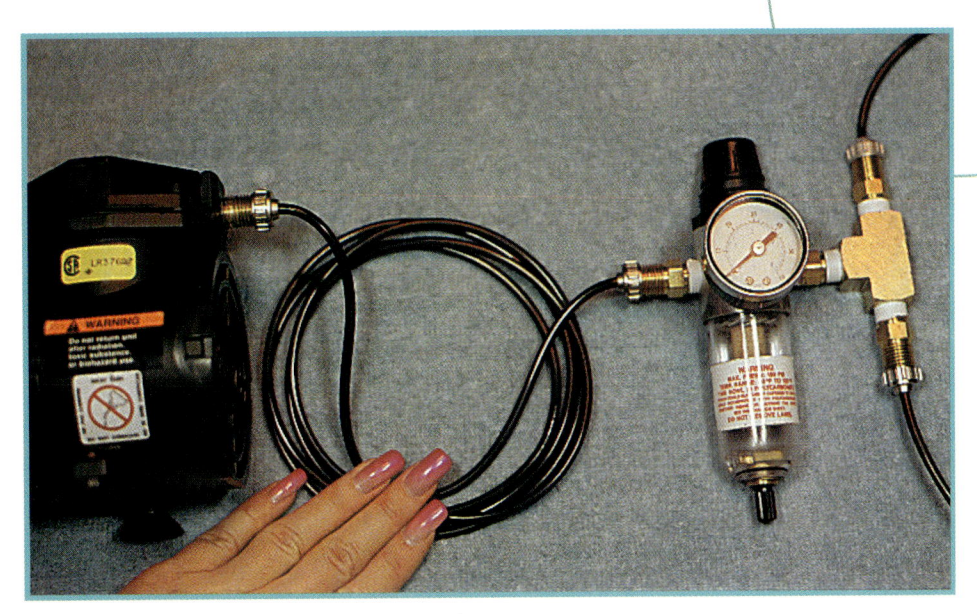

FIGURE 2-6: Plastic hose between compressor and moisture separator.

There are small **in-line moisture traps** available too. I have found these traps to be inadequate in many salon environments and high humidity areas. However, I have known a few artists in high humidity areas who have used them as a second moisture barrier on their airbrush hose connected to their airbrush.

Adapters

There are a number of adapters on the market to assist in attaching different size **air hose couplings** (threaded part of air hose which attaches to compressor or airbrush) to your compressor or airbrushes. Most manufacturers create a custom size air valve so only their airbrush will fit on the hose. Some compressors have unique size fittings that will require an adapter to fit your air hoses to it. These adapters are available through airbrush manufacturers, their distributors, and sometimes a good hardware store will be able to help you out.

There are specialty fittings designed to eliminate threading fittings together. These fittings are called **quick connects** (or **disconnects** depending on the manufacturer). These fittings are attached to the airbrush and the hose. The airbrush has a male end which is pressed into the female end attached to the air hose. To release the airbrush, one pulls on the sleeve on the air hose attachment and the airbrush is "popped" out of the hose. The female hose attachment has a shut-off valve so when the airbrush is removed, no air will escape. Larger quick connects are available for the other end of the air hose and compressor.

Manifolds

Many times you will desire to connect more than one airbrush and air hose to one compressor or compressed gas cylinder regulator. This is achieved by using an air hose **manifold**. The air hose manifold is available ready-made through your distributor, manufacturer or you may assemble them with parts from a hardware store.

The **T-manifold** or **T-junction** permits the artist to connect two airbrush hoses. Attach the T-manifold to the moisture separator if attaching to a compressor. (Figure 2-7) Always use Teflon tape between two metal surfaces being threaded together, to prevent air seepage. You now may connect two airbrushes to the manifold. Some manifolds have an on and off screw to close the opening if only one airbrush is attached. If you do not have this feature, you must always have two airbrushes connected to operate the compressor. If you are using a compressor designed to operate only one airbrush, you may connect the T-manifold and attach two airbrushes, but you may operate only one at a time.

The Tri-manifold or Cross-junction allows the artist to attach three airbrushes to one compressor. Attach the tri-manifold to the moisture separator if attaching to a compressor. Always use Teflon tape between two metal surfaces being threaded

FIGURE 2-7: The T-Manifold attached to the moisture separator.

together, to prevent air seepage. You now may connect three airbrushes to the manifold. Some manifolds have an on and off screw to close the opening if only one or two airbrushes are attached. If you do not have this feature, you must always have three airbrushes connected to operate the compressor. If you are using a compressor designed to operate only one airbrush, you may connect the tri-manifold and attach three airbrushes, but you may only operate one at a time.

The Multi-Manifold or multiple outlet hose adapter allows the artist to attach four or more airbrushes to one compressor. The multi-manifold is assembled by connecting t-manifolds and cross-manifolds to build a manifold to attach the desired number of airbrushes. Attach the multi-manifold to the moisture separator if attaching to a compressor. (Always use Teflon tape between two metal surfaces being threaded together, to prevent air seepage. You may now connect your airbrushes to the manifold. Some manifolds have an on and off screw to close the opening if only one or two airbrushes are attached. If you do not have this feature, you must always have an airbrush attached at each outlet to operate the compressor. If you are using a compressor designed to operate only one airbrush, you may connect the multi-manifold and attach all your airbrushes, but you may only operate one at a time.

Chapter 3

Airbrush Paint and Supplies

When you have decided on your airbrush equipment, the next step will be to stock up on airbrush paint and supplies you will need to complete the airbrush nail color service. Many times, when you purchase your airbrush, you will have the chance to purchase an airbrush nail system. I recommend buying a system designed for working on nails, not a hobby or craft kit for airbrushing. A hobby or craft kit will not include the correct accessories and products for airbrushing nails. An airbrush system for nails should be available from your professional beauty supplier and include all the proper supplies for airbrushing nails that you need to get started. You may add additional paint colors and design tools as you become more proficient.

FIGURE 3-1: Airbrush paints and supplies.

Airbrush Nail Paint

There are a number of water-based acrylic paints that may be used for airbrushing nails. At this time, most airbrush paint sold for airbrushing fingernails was originally manufactured for other purposes and is sold into our industry (sometimes repackaged in bottles saying it is for the nail industry) as another use of this paint. As I was writing this book, I became aware that the first paint was being created specifically for use on natural and artificial nails!

Whatever you use, be certain that the manufacturer of the airbrush paint you are using has clearly stated on the paint bottle or in literature that this paint may be used for airbrushing nails. Keep this information in your Hazard Communication Standard (HCS) File. Every salon who has employees is required by **OSHA** law to have a HCS File. In this file, keep your **MSDS Sheets**, product ingredient lists and information stipulating that this product is recommended for use on fingernails. This insures the manufacturer's liability is intact when using the product per manufacturer's directions.

If the paint you are using does not clearly stipulate it may be used on fingernails, you may send a registered letter to the manufacturer requesting a letter for your file. Ask them to clearly stipulate in the letter that their paint may be used for airbrushing nails. If you do not receive a letter from the manufacturer of the paint, I would not use this paint to airbrush nails, since you do not have manufacturer's liability.

You must use a water-based acrylic paint on nails. Different brands of paint will look and last differently on the nails, especially on natural nails. I recommend testing different brands of paint to see which works best for you and your clients. The paint will be sealed to the nails by using a type of nail polish compatible with the paint and the client's nails. If the polish is not compatible, the paint will shrink or crack, giving it an alligator skin or textured appearance. If the paint is still wet when the polish is applied, it may produce a similar result. Be certain your paint is dry before protecting it with clear nail polish.

There are a few types of airbrush nail paint that are available. The most common airbrush nail paint type is an opaque paint which has complete coverage. The next type of paint is a transparent paint which is a see-though color. These two terms are explained more thoroughly in the chapter on Color Theory. There are pearlescent paints which have a metallic or reflective particle added to the paint to impart a frosted or metallic look. The pearl particles are most often white, although gold and opalescent flecks are used. Opalescent paints have a pink, lilac or blue reflective particle or a combination of different color pearl particles for a unique finish. Other colors may be available. Pearlescent paints are available in opaque for coverage or transparent to add a shimmer or highlight to a nail color when the nail is moved at an angle to the light.

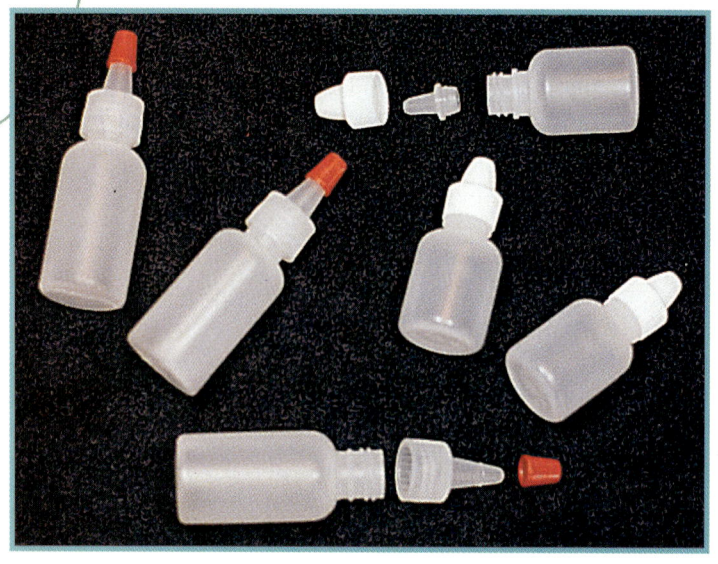

FIGURE 3-2: Dropper bottles and squeeze bottles.

Empty Paint Mixing Bottles

One of the best-selling features of airbrushed nail color is the fact that you can mix custom colors to match fabrics or nail polishes. You will require empty mixing bottles for this purpose. The most common and attractive sizes are the 1/3 ounce dropper bottle and 1/2 ounce squeeze bottle. (Figure 3-2) I recommend using these bottles for all your paints, since most airbrush nail paints come in larger, unattractive bottles which are difficult to store at your station. The small empty bottles fit perfectly in a polish display rack and appear more professional. Many nail airbrush paints are multi-purpose and do not have a professional look for your nail table. Store the large airbrush paint bottles in your back room and fill your small mixing bottles for your station from the larger bottles.

Aerosol Nail Paint

There are some **aerosol nail paints** on the market which you may use with different design stencils and tools. These paints offer an inexpensive way to try some basic nail painting techniques that do not require the investment in airbrush equipment. The aerosol paints are adequate for simple designs, color blends and traditional French manicures. However, the aerosol paints do not offer the control and precision in designs that you will have with an airbrush.

Airbrush Paint Cleaner

Use the airbrush paint manufacturer recommended **airbrush paint cleaner**. This will maintain your manufacturer's liability. If the manufacturer does not have its own airbrush paint cleaner, contact the manufacturer and request an answer in writing for the proper airbrush paint cleaner to use for their airbrush paint. Store the written or faxed response in your HCS File.

When using your airbrush paint cleaner, follow manufacturer directions for cleaning the airbrush. If your product is a concentrate, it may recommend different dilutions for cleaning the airbrush, soaking parts and possibly cleaning the skin. Some products are safe for use on your client's hands and feet for cleanup after the airbrush nail color application. Some manufacturers may recommend another product for skin cleansing. I recommend using a squirt bottle for dispensing your airbrush cleaner into the airbrush.

DO NOT USE WINDOW CLEANER OR AMMONIA AS AN AIRBRUSH PAINT CLEANER in your airbrush or on your customer's hands. You may use it to clean inanimate surfaces like your table top or plastic stencils. Be sure to rinse those surfaces well prior to contact with skin.

If skin contact occurs, the skin should be flushed with water. Contact a doctor if irritation develops. Many people are sensitive to the ingredients in window cleaner and will have an allergic reaction to an airbrush cleaned with window cleaner or if the skin is cleaned with window cleaner. By using window cleaner in this manner you are clearly not following the manufacturer's directions and have no manufacturer's liability. If your client sues you for an allergic reaction, you have used a product that was not recommended for use on your client's skin. Your insurance company may settle the lawsuit, but you have behaved unprofessionally and have jeopardized your future insurability. Ammonia is an irritant to skin, eyes and your lungs. You may be jeopardizing your own health as well as your clients.

Airbrush Color Base Coat and Protective Coats

In order to create long-lasting nail color with an airbrush, you must use the right airbrush nail paint and nail polish products to seal it to the nail. Most airbrush nail paint manufacturers offer a sealer that works well with their airbrush paints. Some nail polishes work better than others. Experiment with different products on your nails or your close friends' nails to see which products work best with your airbrush nail paints and other nail products.

Always Use A Nail Polish Base Coat Under Airbrushed Nail Color. Many airbrush nail artists do not use a base coat of nail polish prior to the application of airbrushed nail paint, especially on artificial nails. I have found that the durability and appearance of the finished nail color will be significantly diminished when no base coat is applied. Using a base coat of polish on *all types of nails* to be airbrushed improves adhesion of the airbrushed paint to the nail. In many cases, I use a special effect base coat to enhance the airbrushed nail color.

BASE COATS ON NATURAL NAILS (FINGERS AND TOES!)

Natural nails require a bit more attention when applying airbrushed nail color as well as traditional nail polish. If you have many natural nail clients, you are aware of how difficult it may be to find a nail polish that lasts well on the natural nail. The natural nail tends to be chemically attracted to different nail polishes. If you have found one that works well for your client, I recommend using the same base coat under your airbrushing. Apply a thin coat of the polish over the entire nail, the nail sides and nail tip. I call this "**bumpering** the nail". By applying your base coat around the side and front edge of the nail, you have sealed the natural nail inside the polish.

After the application of the base coat, you may apply a special effect polish. I use a **crystalline base coat** that has small white crystals in it. The crystalline base coat is similar to a pearl or frost traditional nail polish, but with better reflective qualities. Many people use **opalescent** or **shimmer** base coats for a similar effect under the airbrushed nail paint. Apply your transparent airbrushed nail color or nail art over the special effect base coat.

After you have completed your airbrushing, it is time to adhere the airbrush nail paint into your base coat. I recommend using a **thin topcoat** or **nail paint bonder**. It is important that the product you use for the first step of sealing the nail paint to the nail is very thin. The thin paint bonder will saturate the airbrushed nail paint and melt it into the base coat. Apply the airbrush nail paint bonder to the nail sides and nail tip, encasing the natural nail inside the airbrushed color. When applying the paint bonder, be sure there is plenty of polish on the polish brush. Let only the liquid on the brush touch the airbrushed nail, use the polish brush as a guide for the liquid down the nail. Avoid using the bristles of the polish brush on the dried airbrush nail paint since this may "scratch" or "move" the airbrush nail paint. Permit the airbrush paint bonder a few minutes to dry.

After the paint bonder has dried, use a thick, **protective nail glaze**. Use the airbrushed nail glaze recommended by your paint manufacturer, not your natural nail topcoat (it's generally too soft-wearing). Since airbrushed nail paint is a thinner coating than traditional nail polish, it will wear off the edges of the nail faster. To prevent this, use a hard-wearing glaze and do a good bumpering of the natural nail free-edge! Some people are fine with one coat of airbrushed nail glaze, but I always apply two coats of the protective nail glaze (especially for clients who work with paper). Be sure to bumper the nail sides and edge with the glaze on each coat. When I am applying the protective nail glaze, I call my customer's attention to how I apply the nail glaze. I show them how to bumper the nails and recommend that they repeat the procedure that night for optimal protection. Natural nail clients should glaze their nails regularly for optimum results. Most airbrush nail glazes dry in minutes. Only guarantee your work when the client uses your airbrush nail glaze, which means they must buy it from you. The topcoats they already have at home may interact with the airbrush paint and ruin it. Some nail technicians include a bottle of airbrushed nail glaze with a client's first set of airbrushed nails.

Natural nails tend to be more flexible than a nail with artificial support such as a sculpture or a wrap. When the natural nail bends, it creates a crack in the nail color. Overtime, this crack will become a chip from repeated movement of the nail, and water and dirt working their way into the crack. This is prevented by regular applications of protective nail glaze by the nail client at home. If the client's airbrushed nails still chip even with good home maintenance, you may need to re-evaluate your base coat and try another.

BASE COATS ON ARTIFICIAL NAILS (SCULPTURES, WRAPS, ETC.)

Artificial nails will wear better than natural nails since they do not have the same flexibility. Nail polish is attracted to the artificial nail product and will last longer. Use the base coat recommended by the airbrush paint manufacturer. Use a clear base coat for French manicures and special effect base coat under transparent airbrush paints. Bumper the nail by applying a thin coat of the polish over the entire nail, the nail sides and nail tip. By applying your base coat around the side and front edge of the nail, you have sealed the artificial nail inside the polish.

After the application of the base coat, you may apply a special effect polish. I use a crystalline base coat that has small white crystals in it. The crystalline base coat is similar to a pearl or frost traditional nail polish, but with better reflective qualities. Many people use opalescent or shimmer base coats for a similar effect under the airbrushed nail paint. Apply your transparent airbrushed nail color or nail art over the special effect base coat.

After you have completed your airbrushing, it is time to adhere the airbrush nail paint into your base coat. I recommend using a thin topcoat or nail paint bonder. It is important that the product you use for the first step to seal the nail paint to the nail is very thin. The thin paint bonder will saturate the airbrushed nail paint and melt it into the base coat. Apply the airbrush nail paint bonder to the nail sides and nail tip, encasing the natural nail inside the airbrushed color. When applying the paint bonder, be sure there is plenty of polish on the polish brush. Let only the liquid on the brush touch the airbrushed nail. Use the polish brush as a guide for the liquid down the nail. Avoid using the bristles of the polish brush on the dried airbrush nail paint since this may "scratch" or "move" the airbrush nail paint. Permit the airbrush paint bonder a few minutes to dry.

After the paint bonder has dried, use a thick, protective nail glaze. Use the airbrushed nail glaze recommended by your paint manufacturer. Since airbrushed nail paint is a thinner coating than traditional nail polish, it will wear off the edges of the nail faster. To prevent this requires a hard-wearing glaze and good bumpering of the artificial nail free-edge. Some people are fine with one coat of airbrushed nail glaze, but I always apply two coats of the protective nail glaze (especially for clients who work with paper). Be sure to bumper the nail sides and edge with the glaze on each coat. When I am applying the protective nail glaze, I call my customer's attention to how I apply the nail glaze. I show them how to bumper the nails and recommend they repeat the procedure that night for optimal protection. Nail clients may glaze their nails when they need it to refresh the shine and nail color. Most airbrush nail glazes dry in minutes. Only guarantee your work when the client uses your airbrush nail glaze, which means they must buy it from you. The topcoats they already have at home may interact with the airbrush paint and ruin it. Some nail technicians include a bottle of airbrushed nail glaze with a client's first set of airbrushed nails.

Design Tools

Many people ask me how they may "freehand airbrush" nail designs. I have to explain that the nail (natural and artificial) is a hard surface which will not absorb the moisture in paint. It is impossible to draw "freehand" pictures on the nail as you can on a T-shirt or canvas. To draw pictures on a shirt or canvas, you bring the airbrush very close to the surface and begin to paint. The fabric absorbs the moisture of the paint and holds the airbrush color in place. Working on the nail is very different. When you bring the airbrush close to the nail and try to draw, the paint released will puddle on the nail and begin to run off. The only freehand work done on nails is solid-color, contouring color and color fades. All designs which require images such as pictures, letters or graphics require a **design tool**. Repeated passes of the airbrush over the design tool will slowly build up nail color to the desired level. The design tool may be removed and the image desired has been developed.

DESIGN TOOLS

	Stencils	Uncut Nail Mask Paper	Pre-Cut Nail Masks
What It's Made of	Plastic, paper or fabric; may also use household objects such as combs.	Clear tacky paper with paper backing.	Clear tacky paper with paper backing.
How It's Used	Placed over nail, airbrush paint sprayed through or over the stencil.	For making own designs; may be cut with backing on or removed and then placed on a piece of glass.	Positive outside piece or negative inside piece. (Positive piece acts as stencil.)

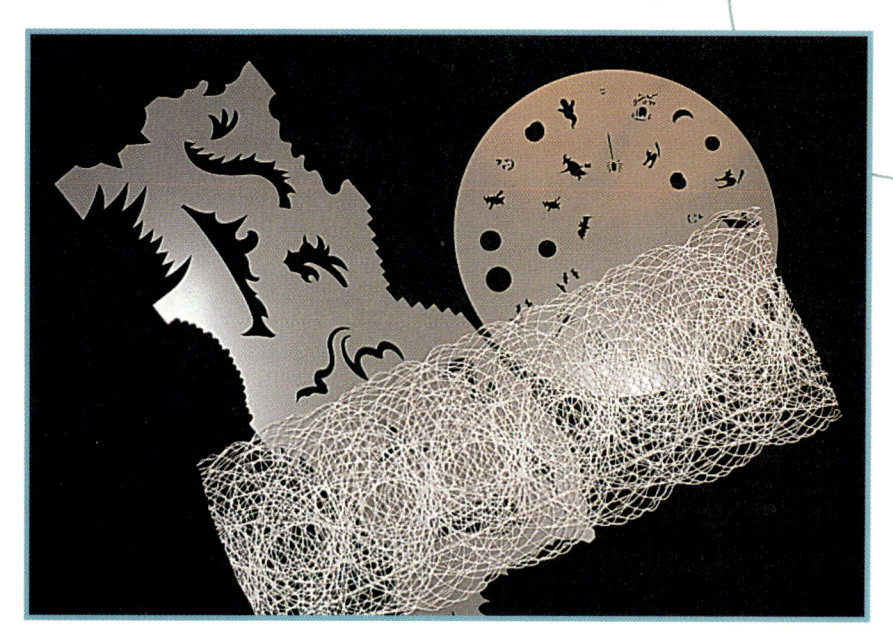

FIGURE 3-3: Stencils are made of plastic, paper, or fabric.

There are a number of materials available to create designs on nails. The most commonly used design tool is a **stencil**. A stencil may be made of plastic, paper or fabric. (Figure 3-3) The stencil has images cut into it or if it's a fabric it has holes in it. The stencil is placed over the nail, airbrush paint is sprayed through or over the stencil. Repeated passes over the stencil will build up the airbrush color. When the image is the color desired, the stencil is removed to expose the new stenciled image on the nail. Many items you have around the house may be used as stencils. Combs, fabrics such as lace and tulle, make fun stencils.

I enjoy cutting my own designs out of nail mask paper (also called frisket paper). Mask paper is a clear tacky paper with a paper backing. You may cut designs out of the mask paper with the backing on for flexible stencils or remove the backing and place the mask paper on a piece of glass to cut out designs. I travel with my glass plates so I keep their dimensions small. I work with a glass plate that is 8″ x 13″ and 1/4″ thick. I place a ruler on the glass to cut striping nail masks (shown in technical 10). The ruler must have a flat back so it may be glued with an appropriate adhesive that you may find at a craft or hardware store. I recommend cutting your popular designs ahead of time (before work, while watching TV or during a cancellation) so you may offer a design without having to take up valuable client time cutting your masks. Use both sides of the glass for storage of your cut nail masks.

There are **pre-cut nail masks** available too. They come in different shapes and designs. There is an inside piece (referred to as a **negative mask**) and an outside

Airbrushing Basics   47

piece (**positive mask**). The negative mask is placed over an area and the area covered by the mask does not change or is inactive. The positive mask acts more like a stencil. The opening in the mask is the active area and the surroundings do not change.

Generally, if the designs travel from the outer edge of the nail on the right hand, they should travel from the outer edge of the nail on the left hand. Many times beginners forget to do this and travel across both hands doing the image exactly the same. The designs on the right hand should be a **mirror-image** of the designs on the left hand. This is demonstrated in technical number 11. Pre-cut masks have the mirror image available for doing quick, precisely cut designs. If you are using a stencil, flip the stencil over and use the other side of the image for the opposite hand to create a mirror image of your designs.

For minor touch-ups or adding quick details I have a stylus with two different dot sizes and small paintbrushes (10/0 + 15/0). I like to put my initials on nail tips that are going to be photographed or displayed so people may immediately identify my work. Many clients like their nails initialed to show that they are wearing custom work from an artist.

Practicing and Displaying Nail Tips

When learning to airbrush nails, you do not require a model to begin practicing. You may practice successfully on plastic nail tips. I use nail tips which are rounded at the top, indicating the cuticle area of a real nail and ideally, ones with no size numbers on the top surface. These nail tips need to be mounted to a surface for stability when airbrushing them (or the spray will blow them away). Some people place putty or double-sided tape on a practice hand or finger and place the nail tip securely into it. Others use double-sided tape on a sturdy board like the side of a corrugated cardboard box or **foam board** (also called **foamcore**). I have seen nail tips glued to the end of orangewood sticks and completed nails placed in flower vases. I prefer to mount a pin to the back of my nail tip with a ball of acrylic or hot glue. When the adhesive is dry, you may pin the mounted nail tip to the foamcore for practice and pin the finished nail on your displays. There are nail tip wheels and other displays available for practice and display of completed work.

After you have completed a nail tip that you like, place it in a display to tempt your clients. I pin my completed nail tips on a black velvet board. The velvet board looks nice on its own, but there is a tray and glass–covered tray that the velvet display case may be placed in for additional protection and appearance. (Figure 3-4) With your completed nail tips mounted on pins, the display may be easily changed for holidays or special events. The nail tips may be placed on other surfaces like a small pillow or fabric–covered picture frame for varied looks.

FIGURE 3-4: Airbrushed plastic nail tips displayed on a velvet board.

If your nail tips are mounted on sticks, try the flower vase display or placing the sticks in sand in a pail for unique looks. If you placed your nail tips on putty or double-sided tape, they may be glued or taped to another type of surface for display. The many pre-fabricated displays available today give you a large selection of displaying your airbrushed nail colors and artwork.

Airbrushing Basics

Airbrush Nail Color Theory

Chapter 4

Introduction to Nail Color Theory

Many people do not realize the importance of understanding color and its influence on your work. Color choices dramatically affect the client who will be wearing them and will make or break a design. I often speak to nail technicians who tell me stories of how beautiful a design was the first time they sprayed it. Then they did the same design on another client, changing a few colors. The design did not have the same impact that it had had the first time. Because they didn't understand color theory, they couldn't interpret what had gone wrong.

There are many theories or methods of using color. If my brief chapter on color theory stimulates your desire to know more, visit the library or book store. There are dozens of books on color theory written by many artists. Some are written to express the methods of the author of that book and others are written as collections of different color theories and how one may apply them. Most successful nail artists will find their own favorite methods of using color, possibly never realizing their instinctual choice of colors. Other nail artists never comprehend why their work doesn't seem to reach out. They may have copied an exact design from someone else, without keeping the same color palette. The lack of knowledge in color theory becomes apparent every time I check out an industry trade magazine's nail art section. Many times you will see a design that strikes you as "uncomfortable" or "unreal" looking due to the placement of a color next to the skin. Sometimes a design lacks the desired impact because of the combination of colors. After you have studied this chapter, pull out one of the industry magazines and review a few nail art sections, especially ones submitted by the readers. You will see what I mean.

LIGHT IS EVERYTHING TO COLOR

Everything we see is the result of light. In the mid-1600's Sir Isaac Newton shined sunlight through a **glass prism**. The light went through the glass prism and shone on the wall as a rainbow. Most of us did this in grade school. For those of us who do not remember, find a piece of crystal or some rhinestones. Place it in the sunlight and you will see colors reflected onto the wall. This discovery showed that light contains color. As a matter of fact, visible light contains the full-spectrum of color represented by the true colors on the outside of the color wheel.

When something appears white to us, what we are seeing is all visible light waves being reflected from a surface. When something appears as a color, we are actually seeing light bounce off a surface, and the color we see is the only color being reflected. When something appears black, all visible light waves are being absorbed by the surface. An easy demonstration of this phenomenon (and the best way I have found to remember it) is our choice of T-shirt color for a hot day in the sun. You learned early on that a white T-shirt is the coolest to wear in the sun. That is due to the fact that the white color of the shirt **reflects** the light from the shirt (which reflects the heat away from your body). If you choose a black T-shirt, you would be very warm because black **absorbs** all visible light waves and the heat from the light.

Selection of lighting is a very important consideration for an airbrush nail artist. You must contemplate what light or lights will be best for choosing and applying airbrush nail colors. You must think about the light that your client's nails (and your nail color or artwork) will be viewed in. Incandescent lighting (traditional round light bulbs) tends to give off a **warm** influence (red through yellow on the color wheel) to your nail colors. If your client spends time under fluorescent lighting (long bulbs in office or retail settings) this will have a **cool** effect (green to blue-violet on the color wheel) on the nail color. Fluorescent lighting seems to pronounce the blue in nail color. When using red-violet nail colors, remember that they tend to get purple under fluorescent lights and that could be a problem for some clients.

There are excellent lights available that are perfect for the nail table. They are usually promoted as lights that are low-temperature and low-glare. I find a warm influence on nail color misleading. I have found that fluorescent lighting works best for me. The fluorescent light keeps me from choosing a color that would be too purple for my client's tastes. Fluorescent lighting also does not heat up my work area.

Another lighting option may be found at your specialty lighting fixture store. There are particular light bulbs available that simulate sun light or natural light to assist in accurate reading of paint colors. Many artists feel they are worth the investment. With a little experimentation, you will discover what works best for you.

The Color Wheel

The color wheel serves as a visual guide on how to use color and how to mix paint colors. First we will examine the **pure colors**. The pure colors are seen around the perimeter or edge of a traditional color wheel. (Figure 4-1) I sometimes refer to the pure color as the **base** or **true color**.

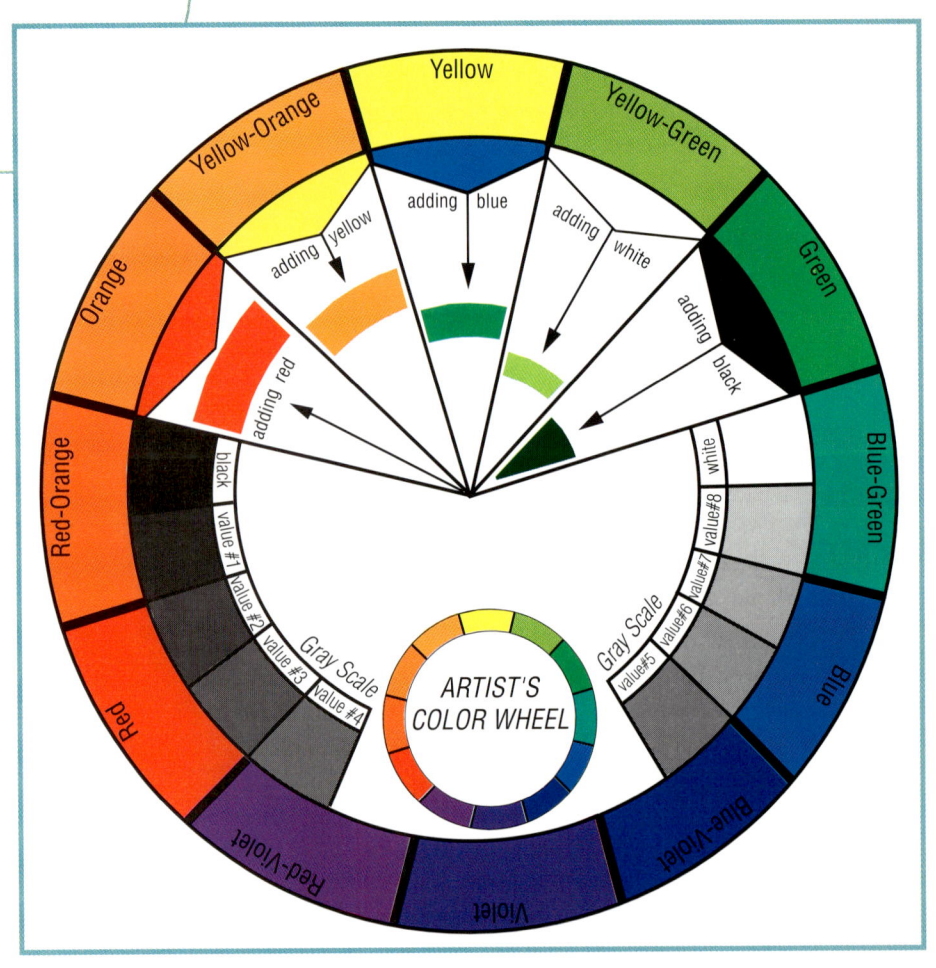

FIGURE 4-1: The artist's color wheel.

- The **primary colors** (also referred to as **basic colors**) are yellow, blue and red. These colors may not be achieved by mixing any other colors. Theoretically, all colors of the wheel may be mixed using one, two or all three of the primary colors.
- The **secondary colors** are green, violet and orange. The secondary color is the result of mixing two primary colors. The combination of blue and yellow create green; red and blue create violet; red and yellow create orange.
- **Tertiary or intermediate colors** are a combination of equal parts of one primary color and one secondary color. When naming these colors the

52 *Milady's Airbrushing for Nails*

primary color name is always placed before the secondary color name. I have listed some common names in parentheses after the intermediate color. Yellow-green (kiwi, lime, chartreuse), blue-green (teal, turquoise), blue-violet (purple), red-violet (magenta, peony), red-orange (scarlet, persimmon), yellow-orange (golden yellow) are the true intermediate or tertiary colors.

When discussing paint, true or pure colors are **transparent**. Transparent color is see-through like a piece of cellophane. When you use a transparent nail color, it will color what is under it permitting any design or other color to show through the transparent color. If the base coat color is **crystalline white** (it has a pearl or reflective quality) and you spray a transparent red over it, you will see the red color with the crystal or frost showing through. (Figure 4-2) If I now sprayed transparent yellow paint over part of the red color, I would see yellow where the nail was still crystalline white, and orange where the yellow overlapped the red! Transparent color will actually mix with another transparent color when the colors overlap. (Figure 4-3) We will use this benefit later in the technical chapters.

The opposite of a transparent color is an **opaque** color. An opaque nail paint will block nail color or a design underneath it. When we start to change our pure colors by adding white, black or gray to them, they become opaque. That means you won't be able to see through them. Opaque nail color is necessary when you want to cover the natural nail or a design color so it won't show through when your nail is finished. If you have a crystalline base coat and spray opaque pink, you will not see the pearl or frost effect where the pink has covered the base coated nail. (Figure 4-4) We will contrast the use of transparent and opaque color in our technical nail designs in later chapters.

Two colors that are traditionally considered opaque are black and white. Some companies make black and white paints for color mixing that are semi-transparent.

FIGURE 4-2: Crystalline white nail with transparent red sprayed over it still shows the white base.

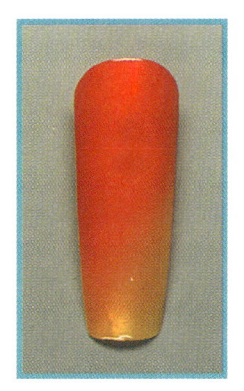

FIGURE 4-3: The same crystalline white nail with transparent yellow sprayed over part of the red.

Airbrushing Basics

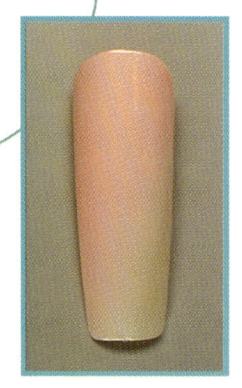

FIGURE 4-4: Crystalline base coat with opaque pink over it hides the base coat.

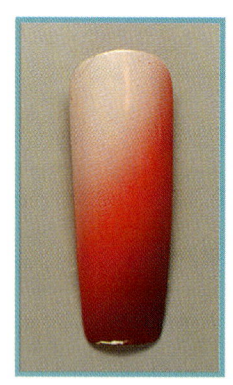

FIGURE 4-5: Tint of red (white added to red paint); the red paint and a shade of red (black added to red paint) sprayed on one nail tip.

If you have an opaque color and wish to have a transparent one, you may add a little water to most products to dilute the concentration of the **pigment** and spray the color more transparently. I suggest using distilled water. Some pigments may react with minerals found in tap water, producing some pungent odors. When you add white to a color, the color is a **tint** of the base color or a lighter color. For instance, if you add white to red paint, it will lighten the red color to a light red, commonly called pink. Pink is a tint of red. When you add black to a color, the color is now a **shade** of the base color or a darker color. If you add black to red paint, it will darken the red color to dark red, sometimes called crimson. To create a tint of a color is to add white to it. To create a shade of a color, you will add black to it. (Figure 4-5)

Ever notice the number of different tints of white! If you have ever painted walls in your home and had to choose the right tint of white, you know what I mean! Where the white is located on the outside of the wheel will determine the true or base color influencing it. Many people prefer a white with a blue or green base for the bedroom walls of a house, since it is a cool relaxing white. In contrast, some people want a warm white (yellow or orange based white like oyster or almond) for the kitchen since it will be a high energy and cozy room.

Just as there are many tints of white, there are many shades of black. If you have ever tried to match two black garments that were not from the same manufacturer or dye lot, you know how different black shades can be. Black has a variety of undertones depending on the base color or the color on the wheel it is closest to. If the black is closest to the red section of the color wheel, you will see a red undertone in the black.

Value is the lightness or darkness of a color. Each section of the color wheel represents a true color. (I sometimes refer to the section as a "piece of the pie," since the sections look like a pie cut into 12 pieces.) The color wheel I like to have my stu-

54   Milady's Airbrushing for Nails

dents fill in has true color placed in the center of each "piece of pie". (Figure 4-6) The lighter this true color becomes, the more it travels to the edge of the wheel towards white. The outside of the wheel represents light being reflected or white in paint terms. The darker the true color becomes, the more it travels toward the center of the wheel to black. The very inside of the wheel represents the absence of light, light being absorbed, or black, in paint terms.

In theory, one should be able to create black by mixing the three primary colors. When mixing paint, this does not happen. When one mixes the three primary colors, you will have a shade of brown. Depending on which primary color you have the most of, you may see an undertone in the brown color, similar to what we discussed regarding black and white. Think of the glass of water you used to clean your paintbrush in when handpainting. After you have rinsed your paintbrush a few

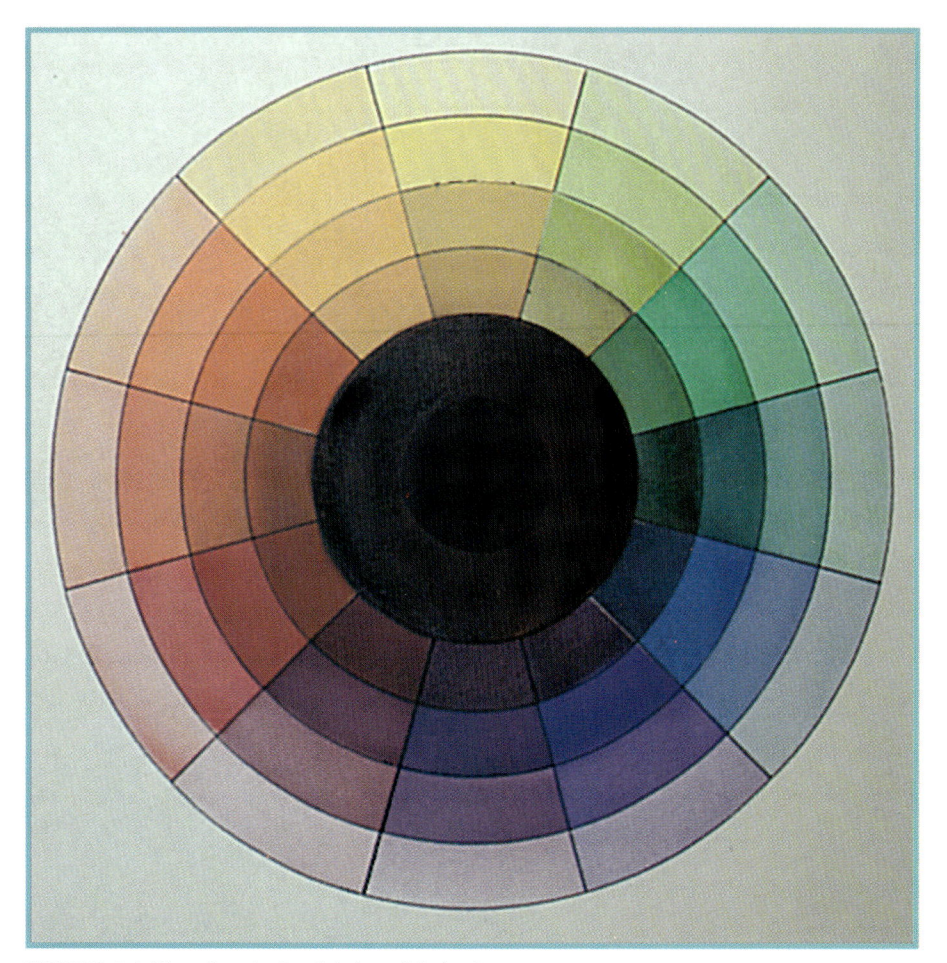

FIGURE 4-6: The color wheel with light and dark values.

Airbrushing Basics

times, the water turns a shade of brown, right? When working with paint, if you mix the three primary colors, you will develop a shade of brown. The color brown surrounds the black as it starts to travel towards the true colors. (Figure 4-7)

When we look at one section of the color wheel (let's use blue), we must recognize that the section represents an infinite amount of colors. The true color traveling toward the edge of the wheel offers a gradation of light values (called tints) of the true color (such as light blue or baby blue). When the true color moves toward the center of the wheel, there is a gradation of darker values (called shades) of the true color (such as indigo or navy blue). Each section of the wheel offers the nail artist a large selection of color.

In addition to running the length of the color section on the wheel, one may choose colors that are changing as they travel towards its neighboring sections or the

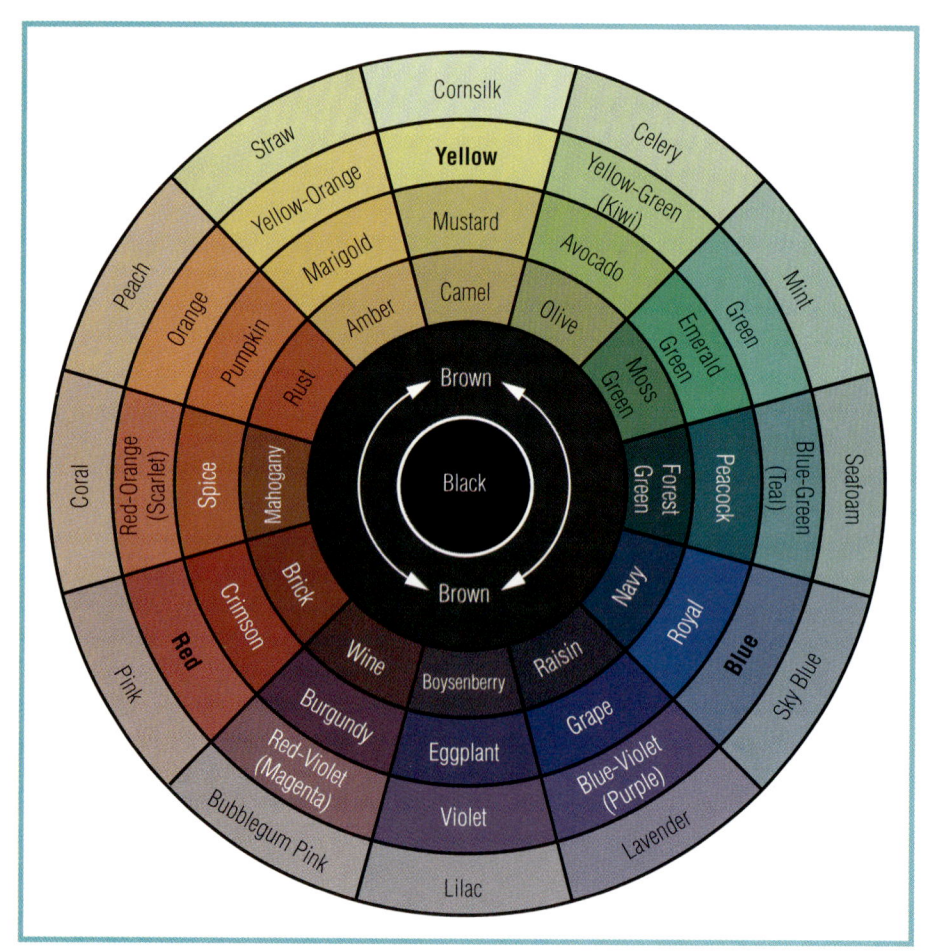

FIGURE 4-7: Colors are darkest toward the center and lighter toward the outer perimeters of the color wheel.

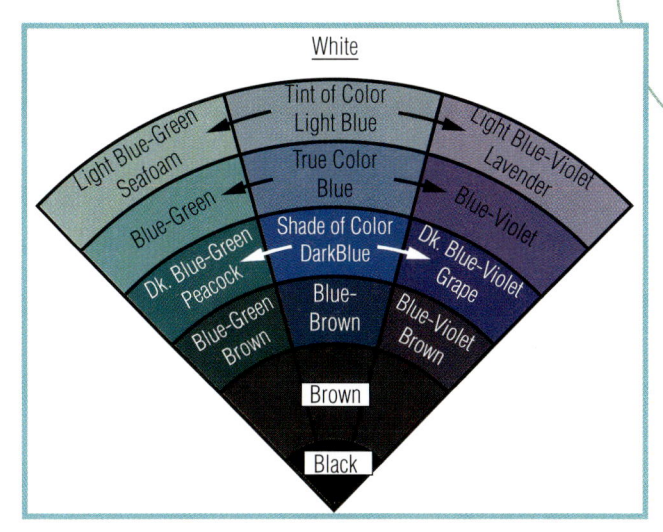

FIGURE 4-8: The true color begins to change as you travel to either side of its section in the color wheel. The true color will be influenced by its neighbor colors as it travels toward them.

width of the section. If we use blue as our example again, blue is true blue when centered in its section of the wheel. When you start to travel sideways towards it's neighboring color, blue-green, the true color blue begins to be influenced by blue-green, until it comes to the blue-green section. (Figure 4-8) Consider the fact that you have all the light and dark values of each color and you have quite an array of color to choose from in just one section of the color wheel.

Color Schemes

A color scheme is the overall mood that your color selection conveys. From the previous section, we learned that we have extensive color choices. One must learn how

SELECTING COLORS

Color Scheme	What This Means	Color Examples
Monochromatic	Single color; generally the preference of the conservative client.	Any one color (pink, red, crimson are all values of **one** color). one color).
Triad of a Color	The true color and the section of color next to it on each side on the color wheel.	Red: red-orange and red violet.
Complimentary Contrast	The combination of a color and the color opposite from it on the color wheel.	Red and green. Also applies to the tint or lighter colors such as pink and mint.

Airbrushing Basics 57

to choose and combine color successfully for each client that will sit in our chair. As we discuss color schemes, I will start to use the term **foundation color** indicating the nail color that the client chooses for their nails or the color we start with when designing a nail. When I have a conservative client that wants a subtle color on her nails, I would use a **monochromatic** color selection. "**Mono-**" means "one" and "**chroma**" means "color"; put it together and it literally means "one color". The most common monochromatic color collection would be to look at red. A light red (pink), true red and a dark red (crimson). Depending on the value of the chosen colors, there may be a subtle or vivid color scheme. (Figure 4-9)

The next type of color selection I would like to discuss is the **triad of a color**. The triad of a color is the true color and the section of color that is next to it on each side. "**Tri-**" means "three". The triad of a color has three sections of the color wheel, three colors which share a common denominator. For example, the triad for yellow is yellow, yellow-orange and yellow-green. Every color on the color wheel has a triad. When choosing color for the average client they usually will be comfortable with colors that are chosen from within the color's triad. Let's say our client loves to wear a scarlet nail color. She would like more variety in her nail color or artwork. We will look to the triad of scarlet or red-orange. The triad for red-orange (scarlet) is red-orange, red and orange. Now I may use these three colors and feel secure regarding my end result. I may use the true color for a vivid color combination or I may choose to use a tint of the true color for a more subtle color combination (Figure 4-10).

The third method of color combinations we will explore is using the **complementary contrast** of a color. The complementary contrast of a color placed next to the chosen color will show the highest intensity of the color. The complementary contrast of each color may be found opposite it on the wheel. For example, let's say

FIGURE 4-9: A subtle and vivid color scheme with red.

FIGURE 4-10: Sample nail tips using the tints and true colors from the triad of red-orange.

your client wants her nails to be very bold and her favorite color is red. By placing a sliver of green color in her nail design with a base color of red will be vibrant. Green and red are opposites on the color wheel. This combination is used often to represent the Christian winter holidays of Christmas. You will see examples of complementary color combinations in most professional presentations, like advertisements or posters—even school colors. The complementary contrasts color scheme will be the color selection you will use for your daring clients who want their nails noticeable from across the room.

The use of complementary contrasts applies to the tint or lighter colors too. Pink and mint, peach and light blue, light yellow and lilac are favorite combinations. These all use the complementary contrast of the base color. The base color of pink is red; the base color of mint is green. Red and green are opposite on the wheel. That is why these colors work so well together. It is not an accident. Much thought and preparation goes into the combination of colors in a design. You will find you will use the complementary contrast color scheme often when doing airbrush nail art.

Say, every time your client is ready for her nail color, she requests scarlet (red-orange); she wants a strong contrast in her design. You would choose the complementary contrast which is blue-green as the best accent color for a vivid design. But using the same color combinations all the time will get boring and you need a larger selection of color. Well, you have it! Using red-orange as our example, we would pick blue-green, the complementary contrast for a vivid look. Since the client is tired of this combination, let's look to the triad of the complementary color for a larger selection of color choices that will contrast well with our design color. This increases our color choices to blue-green, blue and green. You may choose to use a tint or a shade of your color selection from the triad to get the most variety and still have the complementary contrast effect. (Figure 4-11)

There is one last color scheme that I want to identify for working with color on nails. By using the triad of the foundation color (red-orange in our last example) that you choose and the triad of the complementary contrast (blue-green in the last example) on the other side of the color wheel, you actually have six colors to chose from every time you design. This gives you hundreds of color combinations to work with every time you sit down to design a client's nails. (Figure 4-12)

There are more types of color-schemes in color-theory books. The ones I have outlined for you here are the ones I have found to work best for designing airbrushed nails. There are others, but they require a better understanding of color and how your paints works. Once you have mastered the concepts presented here, you may consider investigating further. Different books and tools will have inconsistent use of phrases. For example, the word intermediate color may be interchangeable with the word tertiary color. This occurs when describing color schemes as well. In some texts the term "triad" refers to a different type of color combination than the one described in this book. It is easy to become confused. I suggest becoming com-

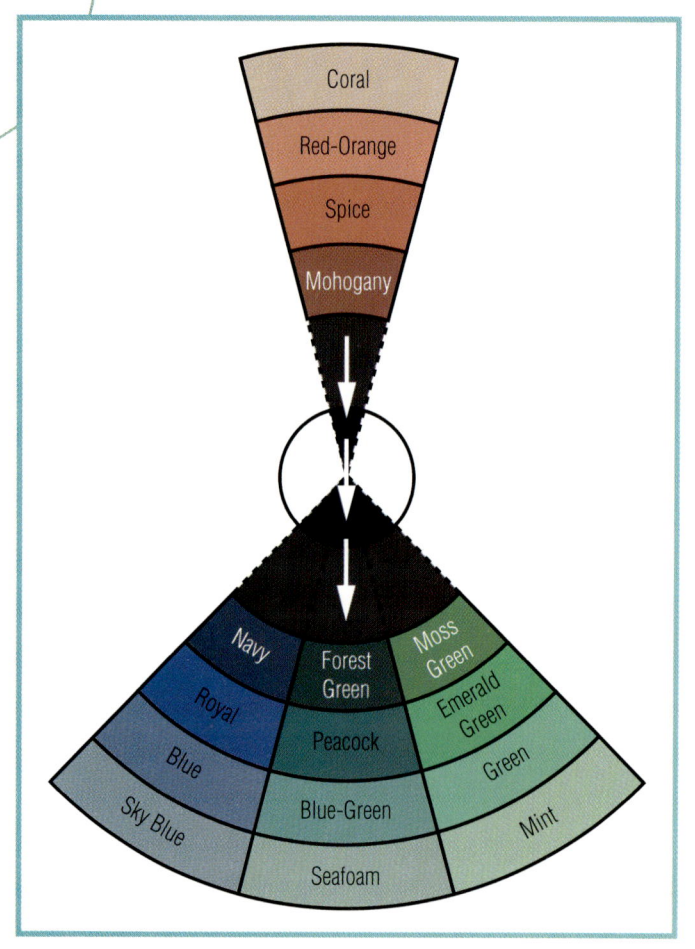

FIGURE 4-11: For a larger selection of complimentary contrast color choices, look at the triad of the complimentary color.

fortable with the color schemes presented in this book before investigating further and getting confused.

One very important thing to remember when designing airbrush nails is *who* decides what colors will be used. From our discussion of successful color selection, you must see that the selection of color should not be left up entirely to the client. Leaving all color choices to the client invites disaster. The client is paying for your expertise and this is where you must exercise control when designing airbrush nails. The client will choose the foundation color most important to them. The client's nature will dictate which type of color scheme you will use. If the client is conservative and has chosen red as the foundation design color, a color fade using pink and red or a monochromatic color scheme would be your choice. If the client is

60   *Milady's Airbrushing for Nails*

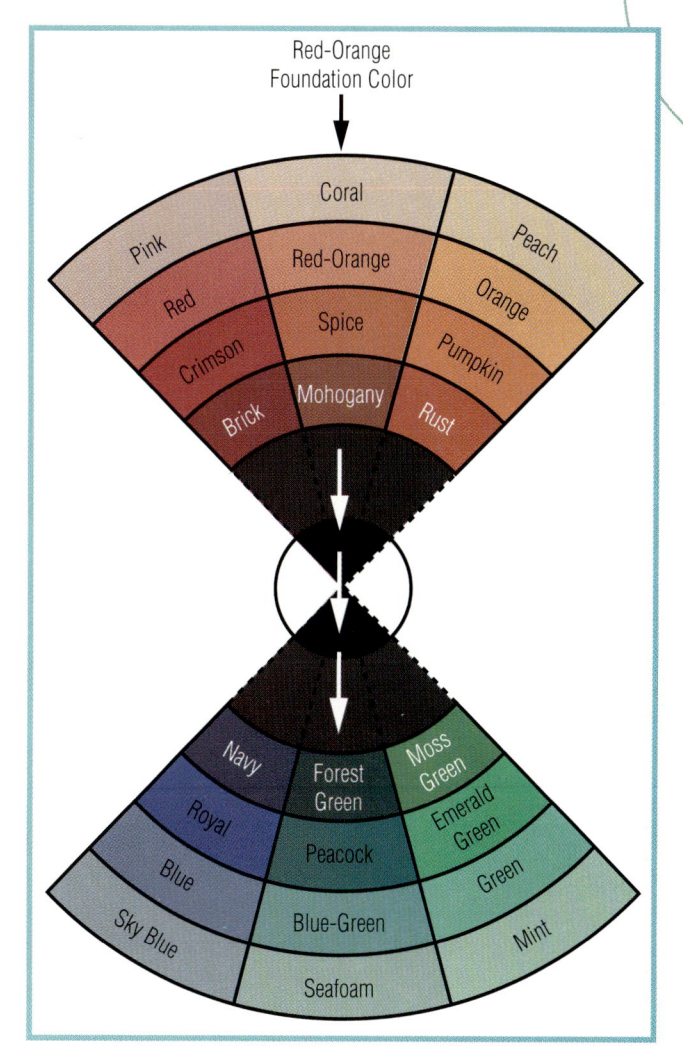

FIGURE 4-12: There are six true colors to choose from each time you design. Use of different values for each color offers hundreds of color combinations.

comfortable with a bit more diversity on her nails, then use the triad of red to create a color fade or design. If the client is bold and wants an airbrush nail design with impact, you can choose colors from the complementary contrasts of the foundation color and the foundation color's triad for your design.

Another important point is to be sure you have your client select the color on your **airbrush nail color display board** that she wishes to wear. I have had many clients tell me that they want to wear a pink. When I choose a few pinks, they are not happy and choose a color I would consider more of a salmon. To be sure no one is confused have them pick their color from your nail color display board and everyone will be happy. A display board is necessary since airbrush paints do not appear the same color in the bottle as they do when sprayed on a nail tip.

Mixing Paint Color

Up to this point we have discussed only how to place paint colors next to each other on a nail for desired effects. Now we are going to shift our focus to how to mix paint colors accurately. One may mix paint colors for the nail in two ways:

1. You may spray transparent nail color onto the nail. Where two colors overlap, you have mixed or created a new color. This new color created by two overlapping transparent colors is called a **transition** color.

2. The second method of mixing new paint colors for the nail would be to use an empty paint bottle and add different colors into the bottle to create a new color paint.

The first step of mixing color is to develop a **paint formula** for each of your new colors. Be sure to keep a record of how much of each paint was added to achieve the desired color. I would suggest designating a notebook for this purpose. I recommend starting with small quantities (drops or teaspoons) of paint when first mixing the new color; the formula may be multiplied when you achieve the desired color. If you happen to create a non-usable color and throw it out, it will not be much paint wasted. When you first start paint mixing, this may happen a few times. Don't let it upset you. Just try to determine where you went wrong and avoid that step when you try again. Once you have mastered those first few challenging colors, you will find yourself addicted to creating new colors for your clients to choose from.

When developing a new color, start by noting the number of drops of each color of paint in your notebook. Then use the slash method next to each color to indicate additional drops of the colors added. When the color is completed, total up the number of slashes, add it to the starting number and you will have a formula that may be multiplied by two or three to fill a paint bottle. Give your new color a name or number to identify it in your notebook and on the bottle. By keeping good records, you will avoid having great colors that will be hard to duplicate exactly when they run out.

When mixing paint colors, you may start with an opaque paint as your foundation color, but you will *always adjust the color with a transparent paint*. Transparent paints do not have an opaquing **medium** or **emulsion** (the liquid that the paint pigment is suspended in) which give opaque colors the ability to cover or block. If you use an opaque color to adjust the color of your paint, this opaquing medium may cause the color to become ash or gray in appearance. The only time you will use an opaque color to adjust a nail paint color is to lighten (white) or darken a color (black).

PAINT TINTS OR LIGHTENING PAINT COLOR

The best mixing technique to start with is to lighten a color or to create a tint of a color. To lighten a color you will add white paint to it. Let's use red as our example. If you have sprayed a nail red and wish to have a lighter red at the tip of the nail, you have two options. First you may mist white paint lightly over the red and develop a pink edge. An easier, more predictable method would be to mix the color pink you would like at the nail tip in an empty bottle. You would take a small quantity of the red paint, say 40 drops, and place it in the empty bottle. Then add five to ten drops of white. Shake up the bottle. If the color is right, you are ready to put it in the airbrush and mist it onto the nail tip. If you would like the color to be lighter, then add small amounts of white paint into the bottle and shake it up until the desired tint of red is reached. Using just red and white paint, one may mix a dozen different tints of red (also called pink). Try mixing a few. Pink is a very popular nail color. (Figure 4-13)

FIGURE 4-13: Mixing red and white paints produces dozens of tints of pink.

PAINT SHADES OR DARKENING A COLOR

The next technique to try is to darken a color or to create a shade of a color. This is achieved by adding a drop or two of black to it. This will work well for a slight deepening of a color. If you have to add a lot of black paint, you may find the color looks **ash** or **gray**. This may occur when the black paint mixes with an opaque color that contains white, which creates gray. In some cases the black paint has an opaquing agent in it to make it opaque and that causes the ash appearance in the paint you are mixing. If this occurs, try picking the darkest foundation color to start with and then adding transparent violet (instead of black) to darken the color. By experimenting, you will find out what works best for you. (Figure 4-14)

FIGURE 4-14: Add black paint to darken red.

Airbrushing Basics

DULL COLORS

To create a tone or a dull color, you will add gray to it. This technique works well when small quantities of gray are added to soften or dull a color. If too much gray paint is added the ash effect described above will result. This technique is limited in use when mixing nail colors. Most people prefer bright, clear nail colors. (Figure 4-15)

FIGURE 4-15: A color becomes dull with the addition of gray.

Develop your paint mixing skills by creating tints, soft tones and shades of the colors you already own. This will create a number of tints and shades of colors that you may use in the different color schemes discussed previously. Having a light, true, dull and dark version of all your colors gives your clients a large range of choices for monochromatic, triad and complementary contrast color schemes.

MUTED COLORS

The complementary contrast of a color is located opposite the color on the wheel. When you mix two colors opposite on the color wheel, all three primary colors are represented. For example, let's look at red. Now find the complementary contrast of red, which is green. What colors make up green? Yellow and blue are the colors that create green. If I mix red and green, all three primaries (red, green = yellow + blue) are present and the mixture will be a shade of brown. If you are unfamiliar with transparent paints, this is a common error when you first start using them. Anytime you overlap two transparent complementary contrasts paints, you will develop a brown **transitional color**. Over a crystalline base coat, this may look bronze and will be attractive in some cases. But if you were after a red and green holiday nail, it didn't work. In order to use transparent complementary contrasts on the same nail, they must not overlap unless you want the third color that develops. To avoid the third color, you must use two opaque complementary colors. If the opaque colors seem to mix a little or do not develop a vibrant contrast, I recommend misting a little white paint between the two colors. (Figure 4-16).

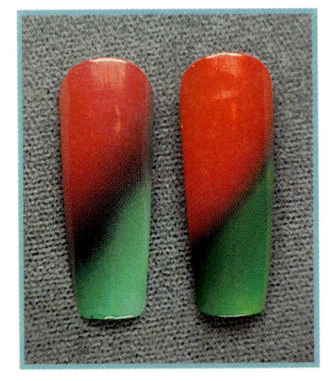

FIGURE 4-16: To avoid brown where the green and red meet, use opaque red and opaque green or mist some white paint in the middle.

64   *Milady's Airbrushing for Nails*

When the complementary contrast of a color is added to the color a drop at a time, it will create a **muted** or less-intense color. Opposite colors on the wheel **cancel** each other out when mixed together. If you add a couple drops of green to red paint it will diminish the vibrancy of the red or cancel the brightness of the red. If you add more green, a brick red (browned-red) will result. If you continue to add green to the red, eventually the end result will be brown.

For example: Let's choose pink as our foundation color to work with. The base color of pink is red. The complementary contrast of red is green. To mute the pink color (or to cancel the vividness of red) you would add transparent green paint. When a drop of green is added to pink, the intensity of the red is muted and the color becomes a softer pink color. You will develop a mauve or browned pink. If it is a light pink it will become a flesh-toned pink, commonly referred to as a French manicure pink. This technique is used for creating muted or less vibrant colors with an earthy feel. The muting technique is employed to develop less-vibrant or flesh-toned colors which are comfortable next to the skin. See the following chart to find out how to adjust colors to create French manicure colors.

Let's try another example: If you have a peach paint and want a muted or flesh-toned peach color, you would add a drop or two of the complementary contrast. Peach is a tint of orange, so orange is our base color. The complementary contrast of orange is blue. If blue is added to the peach paint, it will become a French manicure peach. You may add white to lighten the color if necessary.

PEARL OR OPALESCENT COLORS

To create a pearl or frosted nail color, add a pearl white **shimmer** to the color. A shimmer is a transparent color with a metallic fleck that reflects light. A pearl paint

DESIRED FRENCH MANICURE COLOR

	Color Paint to Start With:	Add: Couple Drops at a Time	To Lighten Add:	To Darken Add:	To Make Semi-transparent
French Pink	True pink	Transparent green	White	Transparent red or red-violet	Distilled water or manufacturer's recommendation
French Peach	Coral or peach	Transparent blue	White	Transparent orange or red-orange	Distilled water or manufacturer's recommendation
French Beige	Brown	Transparent red or red-orange to warm color	White	Brown	Distilled water or manufacturer's recommendation
Bone Nail Tip	White	Brown transparent red to warm	White	Brown	
Ivory Nail Tip	White	Brown + transparent yellow	White	Brown	

Airbrushing Basics

may be created in two ways. If you don't use the color often, you can spray the nail first with the color, then with the pearl white shimmer. I call this the **spray-mix method** for creating new colors. If you use the color often, I recommend mixing equal parts of the color and the pearl white shimmer. After testing the color, you may add more pearl or color depending on the results. This method will be referred to as the **bottle-mix method** for creating new paint colors. The results will be the same; the bottle-mix method is a quick application, the spray-mix method works for quick custom nail color when there isn't much use of this combination (or you don't have an empty bottle handy).

Other metallic finishes or special effects are a gold shimmer or an opalescent shimmer. Some paint companies call these types of paint **interference colors**. The most common opals used in traditional nail polish are pink opal, lilac opal and blue opal. With airbrush paint, these shimmers and opals may be used alone over a color to add a metallic finish (spray-mix), they also may be pre-mixed in a bottle for a faster application of favorites. You can also combine shimmer paints and apply them over a color or mix them in with a color.

For example, a red color with a gold shimmer is popular, especially during the winter holidays. Here are three suggestions for mixing this color combination:

1. You may spray the nails with the opaque red paint, then finish with a mist of the gold shimmer for a red gold nail color. The advantage with this method is you may mist more gold at the cuticle area or nail tip for a "splash of gold" effect.

2. If this red gold nail color is a favorite among your clients, an all over red-gold nail color may be achieved by mixing the colors in an empty paint bottle. The formula would start with opaque red paint in an empty bottle and then adding an equal amount of gold shimmer paint. Shake to blend the color. Spray a sample nail tip to check if you have achieved your desired results. This color may be adjusted to your preference by adding more of one or the other paint.

3. Another method of custom-blending a red gold nail color would be to blend more than one metallic shimmer into the opaque red. Add a combination of pink opal and gold shimmer to the opaque red using the spray-mix method (Example #1) or the bottle-mix method (Example #2). (Figure 4-17)

FIGURE 4-17: Examples of a red nail with different shimmers added; Left nail has pearl white shimmer, center nail has gold shimmer, and right nail has gold and pink opal shimmer.

Milady's Airbrushing for Nails

Color Matching

PAINTS TO FABRIC

After you have custom-blended a few paint colors for your clients, you will be ready to **color-match** paints for your clients. Clients will bring in a swatch of fabric for a special event. Take the swatch of fabric and compare it to your nail color display board. Pick the nail paint that comes closest to matching the fabric color. Examine the nail paint to decide what needs to be changed for the paint to match the fabric. In most cases you will feel that the paint has too much blue or orange, and that it is too light or too dark. To cancel blue or orange, you would add the complementary contrast or the color opposite on the wheel to the paint. To lighten the color we would add white or to darken we would add black.

Let's say the fabric is a soft pink. You will have a number of pink paints to choose from on your nail color display board.

1. Select the nail tip color that is closest in color to your fabric swatch.
2. Examine the paint and determine if the pink color is more blue or orange than our fabric swatch. If our paint is more blue then the fabric, We will put some (say 40 drops) of the pink color we have chosen into an empty paint bottle. We will add the complementary contrast of blue a drop at a time to cancel the blue from the paint. The complementary contrast of blue is orange. Add orange to the paint mixture a drop at a time.
3. Shake the mixture up and spray onto a sample nail tip. When you are close to a color, you must spray it onto a sample nail tip to see if you have matched the color. (Remember, paint does not look the same in a bottle as it does when misted onto a nail.) Repeat this procedure until you have a color match.

Color-matching fabrics becomes easier with practice. This is a service that you should charge a small fee to offer. Time is money. Your client will be thrilled with a perfect match for her special event outfit. Post a sign that you offer this service and recommend bringing the fabric swatch in early so you may work on your custom-blending prior to starting or after your scheduled work day.

TRADITIONAL NAIL POLISH

Ever have a nail polish company discontinue a nail color that was a favorite? Now you may color-match any nail polish color using the same technique described for fabric matching. I recommend matching your popular nail polish colors in addition to any discontinued items. This way you may airbrush all your nail color for your clients and they may purchase the traditional nail polish as a retail item for home maintenance.

1. Polish a nail tip with the traditional nail polish color you wish to match.
2. Find the sample nail tip from your nail color display board which is the closest match.
3. Determine the difference between the two colors. Orange or blue? Lighter or darker?
4. Adjust the color by adding the transparent complementary contrast; lighten the color with white; darken the color by adding black; soften the color by adding gray.
5. If there is a pearlescent or opalescent shimmer, these may be added as necessary.
6. Spray a nail tip with the final color to determine match; nail tip will serve as a new addition to your nail color display board for future reference.
7. Be sure to keep a record of the formula for the new color in your notebook.

Cool and Warm Color Undertones

The colors on the wheel are sometimes broken into different categories. One common way of categorizing a color would be to define it as a cool or warm **hue**. The colors from green to violet on the color wheel, especially blue, and all the shades of gray are known as cool colors, perhaps because they remind us of peaceful settings like water, green pastures, snowy hills or cold icicles. Cool colors have been shown to have a relaxing effect on the human brain: they slow down the metabolism and are commonly used for environments that normally would be stressful. Most medical and dental facilities have changed their waiting rooms to cool, relaxing colors. When decorating your home or office, cool colors are ideal surroundings that are conducive to rest and harmony.

Warm colors are the hues from red to yellow on the color wheel. Warm colors are bright, aggressive and make us think of heat. Red, yellow and orange make one think of fire and the heat of the sun. Warm colors attract the eye and excite the emotions. Warm colors have been shown to excite the brain and raise motivation. Warm colors on advertisements, educational materials may encourage one to study the information closer, pay attention to it.

Every color on the wheel may have a warm or a cool undertone. Think about our ever popular nail color, red! If you had to describe the different types of red nail polish you had, you would describe them as red-orange or red-violet (blue), right? Even though red is normally considered a warm color, it does have a cool side when it has blue undertones. This is true for every color on the wheel. Examine your nail color display board. Mentally note which colors have cool undertones and which colors have warm undertones.

Many beauty companies have taken this color categorizing a step further and offer color analysis. Color analysis is whole book unto itself. You may wish to check one out at the library or order one from your book supply for future reference. Briefly, a color analyst would help a client find what colors are best suited to enhance the client's appearance. Most people will look better with one or the other undertone next to their skin. Some people analyze themselves or sometimes are told they are cool or warm undertoned. If someone comes to you and insists that they must wear certain colors, by all means, accommodate them. Over time, when you have mutual professional trust, if you really feel the client should evaluate a differ color scheme, she will more readily accept your professional advice.

I studied color analysis and offered it as a service for my clients when I had my salon. I found most people do have an innate sense of what colors looked best on them. I found breaking the clients into four categories (as the four seasons—summer, spring, winter and autumn) was a bit controversial. I found it easier to stay with the two common categories of cool skin (green to blue) undertones or warm skin (orange to yellow) undertones to help them pick their best color schemes. If you do not feel confident distinguishing between a cool or warm skin tone, I have two simple questions that usually will give you direction. First, I ask if they prefer a bubblegum pink (cool) or a peach (warm) color on their nails or as a garment worn near the face (Blouse or scarf). Second, I show them two red nail colors (one is a red-orange and the other is a red-violet) and let them choose which they would prefer to wear if they were to wear red. Clients with cool undertones tend to pick the cool colors (red-violet) and clients with warm undertones tend to pick the warm colors (red-orange). This works most of the time!

Color Placement on the Nails

Most clients are more comfortable when traditional nail polish colors are placed on the nail next to their skin. Deep violets, blues, greens and yellows are wonderful design colors but look "unnatural" next to the client's skin. Most clients will be uncomfortable with those colors touching their skin. When you wish to use the deep violets, blues, greens and yellows, place them on the free edge of the nail or in a design which travels through the body of the nail without coming into contact with the cuticle. (Figure 4-18) However, like most "rules" this one will be broken when you have that one client come in for St. Patrick's Day and wants her nails green! Learn what is comfortable for your clients. Remember, as a general rule they will prefer oranges, reds, pinks, red-violets next to their skin. For photography and nail art competition, I would strongly encourage you to follow this guideline. (Go find your Reader Nail Art Sections in one of our trade magazines and see what I mean!)

When designing a nail design, use colors which do not look like a diseased (mold green, brown or mustard yellow) or bruised (purple, blue and black, especially next

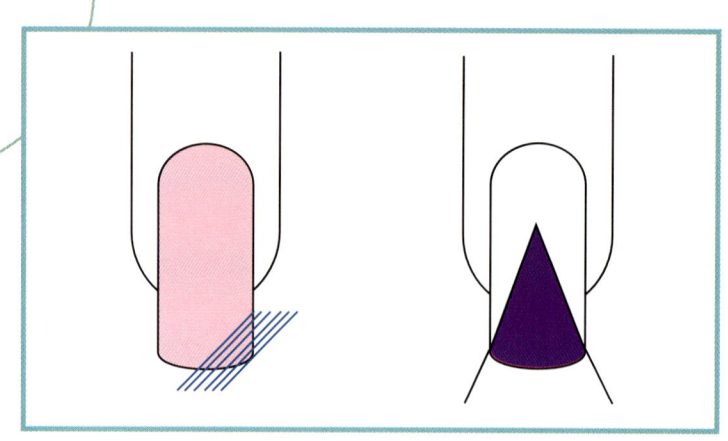

FIGURE 4-18: Non-traditional nail polish colors like yellow, green, and blue should be applied in nail designs to nail areas not touching the skin. Use diagrams as a guide.

to cuticle) nail from a distance. I remember attending a show where they had an airbrush nail competition. One of the competitors chose an army fatigue pattern for the nails using moss greens and browns. While the model was wearing army fatigues, the design was acceptable. However, later that night she attended some after-show parties in a striking red dress. Almost everyone was doing a double take on her nails —not because they were attractive! The red of her dress accentuated (contrasted) the "greenness" of her nails. They looked like she had a massive nail infection!

Another consideration when choosing nail colors is the amount of pigment in your client's own skin. As a general rule, if the skin is light, keep to light, soft colors directly next to the skin. Darker skin tends to have a larger selection of nail colors, including darker colors. Again, this rule is often broken, so you must get to know your client's preferences. Some light-skinned clients love the contrast of light skin and dark red "vampire" nails. I have had many dark-skinned African-American clients who prefer a light beige French manicure with a bone-color free edge. Work within your client's comfort zone if you want to keep them as a client.

Color theory seems like an overwhelming amount of information to remember while designing nails. During our practice in the upcoming chapters on airbrush techniques for nails, we will review this material for each design step. After a while, this will become a natural part of the successful process of airbrush nail color and nail art for your clients.

Chapter 5

Getting Started and Finished

Set Up and Practice

Now it is time to get started. When you first begin practicing, you will need a table, good lighting, comfortable chair, your airbrush equipment and supplies. Prepare a number of nail tips to be airbrushed by mounting them to a surface and base coating them. Assemble your airbrush, hose and compressor per the manufacturer's directions. Place your airbrush paints and airbrush polishes in an accessible tray, roll cart, drawer or polish rack. Have your design and cleaning tools in a tray, drawer or roll cart, ready for use. Put your airbrush cleaner in a squirt bottle. If your airbrush cleaner is a concentrate and must be diluted with water before use, I recommend putting the correct amount of water in the bottle first, then adding your airbrush cleaner concentrate. This will prevent the airbrush cleaner from foaming up.

I set up a cleaning area off to the side of my work area. Either side is fine as long as it is comfortable for you. The best setup is to have a separate roll cart for all of your airbrush nail equipment and supplies storage. Use a drawer that is at a comfortable height for you while you are sitting at the work table. Pull out the drawer and line it with terry or paper toweling. Place your cleaning station, the plastic tray or jar, into it. If you are using an open tray, bowl or jar, I recommend placing absorbent material at the bottom to prevent your overspray from bouncing off the bottom surface of your container and spreading all over. Place your cleaning brushes, airbrush cleaner bottle and other cleaning items in the open drawer. If you do not

PRACTICE TECHNIQUES

Material	Practice Tips and Techniques	What You Learn
Absorbent Paper	Dots, lines, grids, boxes of color	Dots help with aim. Lines widen and soften with distance of airbrush from paper. Boxes of color help you achieve even coating of color.
Nail Tips	Place tips 2–3 inches apart on practice surface. Work on five tips at a time. Don't apply too much, or work too closely.	Lets you practice as if working on client's hand.

have a separate surface to work on off to either side, then use one of the drawers in your nail table, or work to one side or the other on your table. Please try to avoid spraying into your wastebasket. I know I started out that way, but it looks very unsanitary and unprofessional.

Begin practicing on absorbent paper. Whenever you first start airbrushing, I recommend placing a few drops of cleaner into your airbrush and spraying it out into your cleaning station. This wets the airbrush inside and your airbrush nail paints will move through the airbrush better. Start spraying onto the paper to become familiar with how your airbrush operates, staying approximately two to three inches from the surface of the paper. The first thing most people notice is that if you are spraying properly, you will not see the airbrush paint leave your airbrush. It will seem to appear magically on the paper in front of you.

To airbrush properly you will move your whole arm up and down, diagonally, or from side to side. Do not move from the wrist. Your wrist must remain straight and relaxed. If you move from the wrist, your airbrush color will be inconsistent in coverage and intensity. This occurs because the airbrush will start out far from the surface, move closer as your wrist straightens out and then further away as your wrist completes the movement. If you find you are moving your wrist, grasp your wrist with your other hand while practicing and consciously move your whole arm. After awhile, your movements will correct themselves and you will be fine.

Practice spraying a consistent row of dots. When the dot appears where you expect it to, you have learned how to properly aim your airbrush. The next practice step is to draw lines. To draw crisp lines, you must have the airbrush nozzle very close to the paper. The further you pull the airbrush away from the paper, the wider and softer the line will become. After experimenting with dots and lines, draw a grid on your paper by drawing horizontal and vertical lines overlapping each other. This will create rows of boxes. Place a dot in each of the boxes. You are now ready to practice the technique used for airbrushing nails.

When airbrushing nails, the distance from the nail will vary according to the type of airbrush you are using. Most people will be two to three inches from the nail surface. On your paper, spray a smooth even box of color by moving your arm back and forth slowly. Develop even color with no lines by moving back and forth over the same area a few times. If you are seeing streaks or lines, and not a smooth even box of color, you are either too close to the paper or you are releasing too much paint at a time. Practice this technique until you can achieve an even coating of color on the paper with no streaks. (Figure 5-1)

Now you are ready to practice on nail tips. Place your nail tips about two to three inches apart on your practice surface. Lightly coat the nail with your airbrush color. Repeated passes over the nail will build up the airbrush nail color. When first learning, most people are impatient and want to see the color right away. If you are too close to the nail tip or release too much paint on the nail surface at a time the airbrush paint will puddle and begin to run off the nail. (Figure 5-2) The first nail tip

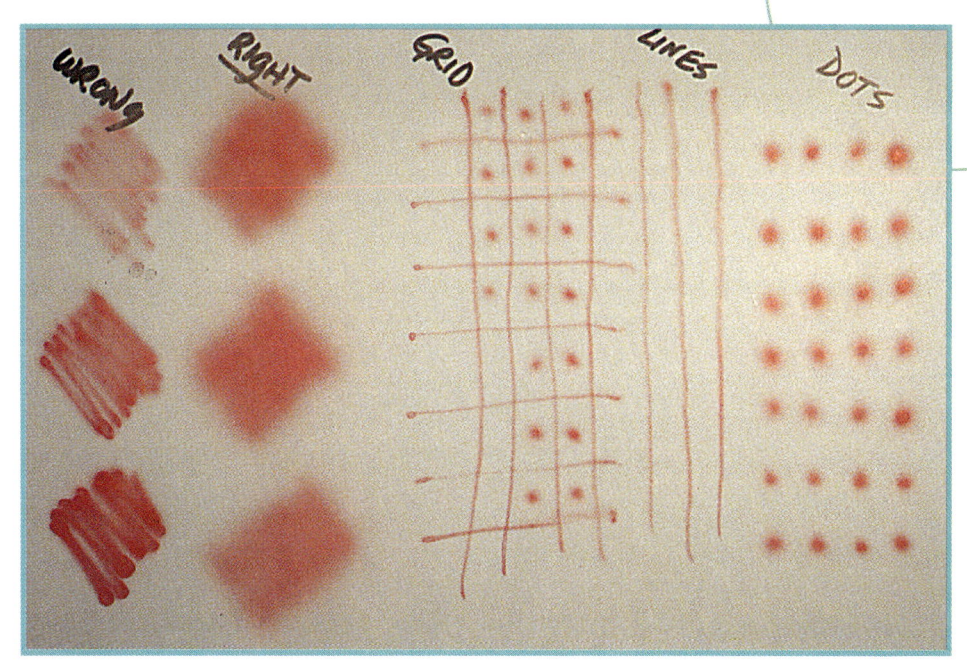

FIGURE 5-1: Practice airbrushing by spraying a grid of lines. Place a dot in the center of each box. Then, try spraying boxes of even color.

is sprayed too quickly or too closely. The second nail tip has the correct, dry appearance.) When correctly applying airbrush nail color, the airbrush paint on the nail should lay down dull, with almost a powdery look to it. If the airbrush paint is shiny or appearing as droplets, wipe the nail tip off and try again. The best way to apply airbrush nail color is to work on five nail tips at a time, as if you were working on a client's hand. Apply one dry layer of color to each nail tip, usually three passes of the airbrush up and down over the nail tip to cover it with color lightly. Move to the next nail tip and repeat the procedure until you have airbrushed each nail tip once. Start with the first nail tip and repeat the procedure on each nail tip until you have reached your desired color. When you have successfully applied the nail color to the five tips correctly, you are ready to move on to the technical chapters on your nail tips. Try the technical chapters in sequence since they become progressively more difficult.

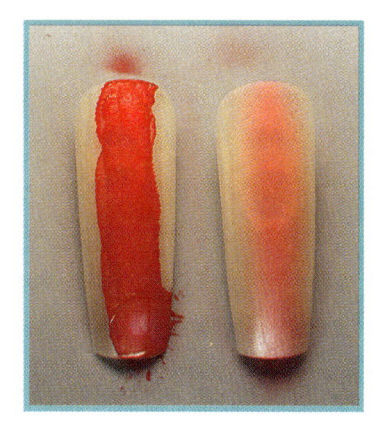

FIGURE 5-2: The nail tip at left shows what happens if you spray too close to the nail tip or release too much paint onto the surface. The paint will puddle and run off the nail. The nail on the right has the correct appearance, achieved by light passes of the airbrush to build up color.

Airbrushing Basics   73

Working on Real People

One of the benefits of adding airbrushing to your services is that you do not require live models to practice your skills. You should become proficient at airbrushing your nail tips, prior to working on live models. After you are skilled at airbrushing nail tips, you are ready to practice on a few close friends or relatives to become comfortable holding the client's hand and cleaning up the overspray when done.

1. Complete your nail service and have the client pay their bill prior to the airbrush nail color service. Have them put on their coat and dig in their pockets or purses for necessary items prior to clean-up.
2. Have the client use a nail brush, and cleanse the hands and nails of any dust or oils from the nail service. Dry the nail and cuticle area thoroughly. Check for droplets of water, missed oils, and dust that would interfere with the airbrush nail color application.
3. Apply the base coat(s) to the nails. Be sure to bumper the sides and the free edge of the nails.
4. Airbrush your client's nails just as you had practiced on the nail tips. I hold my client's hand in mine. My hand encircles each finger as I spray it. My hand catches the overspray as I work so it doesn't fall onto the other nails of my

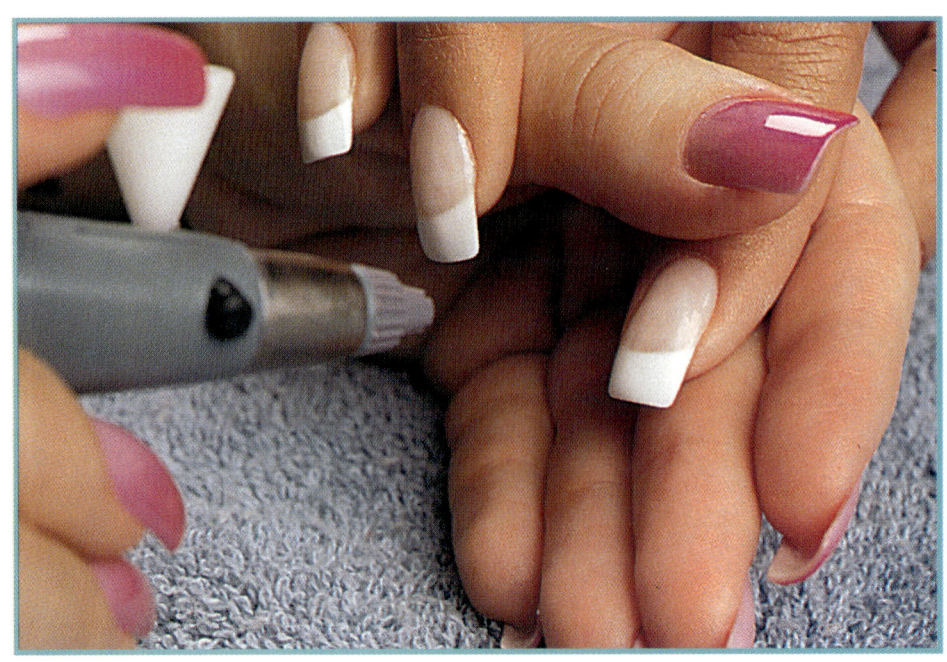

FIGURE 5-3: By holding your client's hand, you can catch the overspray and lessen the amount of clean-up time on her hand.

Milady's Airbrushing for Nails

client's hand. I place my thumb on her finger just above the cuticle area. Overspray lands on my thumb and not on her finger. This reduces cleanup on your client. (Figure 5-3) I use a similar procedure when airbrushing toenails. The paint washes off your hands with airbrush paint hand cleaner, when you sanitize before your next client.

5. Apply your paint bonder or thin top coat to the dry airbrush nail paint. Keep your polish brush parallel to the nail, guiding the liquid down the nail. Do not use the bristles of the brush since this may scratch or drag the paint. Be sure to have enough bonder on the polish brush; a dry polish brush or bristle may also damage your paint. Apply paint bonder to all ten nails. Be sure to saturate all the paint and to bumper the sides and free edge of the nails.

6. Airbrush paint that is not sealed to the nail may be washed away later. Allow paint bonder to dry two to three minutes. I usually clean my airbrush and put it away at this time.

7. Apply one or two coats of protective airbrush nail glaze. Be sure to bumper the sides and free edge of the nails. While applying the protective glaze, instruct your client on proper home maintenance of their airbrushed nail color or nail art. Allow clients to dry their nails for ten minutes.

8. Cleanse the fingers or toes per manufacturer's directions. This may be accomplished at the nail table or pedicure station. Some airbrush skin cleaner products may be used at a sink. Have the client pat her hands or feet on a towel to dry her skin, but avoid pressure on nails for another ten minutes. The airbrush paint bonder may dry tacky and will collect lint if wiped with a towel. Use an orangewood stick or cotton-wrapped implement saturated with polish remover to remove any paint sealed to skin by paint bonder or protective nail glaze.

    **I have found that airbrush nail color artists vary in their client skin cleaning procedures. Some nail technicians cleanse the airbrush paint on the skin after the paint bonder is applied and allowed to dry. Others send their clients home with a small container of airbrush paint skin cleanser for use at home after the color has dried. Experiment with different procedures, to find which one works best for you.

9. You may apply a quick-dry product if desired. For clients in a hurry, I prefer to spray on an oily quick-dry product to avoid damage. Use spray-on products instead of brush-on products for proper sanitation and less-risk of damage to the airbrushed nail service.) Airbrushed nail color is usually surface dry in ten minutes, and completely dry within a half hour since only clear nail polish is applied.

10. Airbrushed nail color will last as well or better than traditional nail polish. Since it is a thinner coating, it tends to be a longer-lasting coating. If you

don't get these results, evaluate your airbrush nail paint and airbrush nail polishes. You may need to experiment with different brands or combinations of products to get maximum durability. Follow manufacturer's directions.
11. Airbrushed nail color is generally removed with regular nail polish remover (acetone will work quickest) unless manufacturer of your paint stipulates otherwise.

In order to offer airbrushed nail color successfully to every client you service, it is necessary to have your airbrush equipment and supplies ready to use at all times. Many people have airbrush systems that are in a box collecting dust. When an opportunity arises for them to use their airbrush equipment, they are not prepared and usually do not have the time to set-up their airbrush system. Having your airbrush system in a roll cart by your side or set up at a nail table/pedicure station offers you the ability to airbrush at a moment's notice, simply by plugging in or turning on your compressor. Airbrushing nail color offers you the ability to make a little more with every client you service all day. For more on how to increase your income and implement airbrushing in your business, read the chapter on marketing.

Chapter 6

TROUBLE-SHOOTING GUIDE

This guide is to be used as a resource whenever you have a problem air-brushing. It includes mechanical and technical problems.

Problem

When the compressor is pumping air and the airbrush trigger is depressed, no airbrush paint comes out. (Figures 6-1, 6-2)

POSSIBLE CAUSE AND SOLUTIONS

1. **No airbrush paint in color cup, paint reservoir or bottle**. Fill airbrush color cup, paint reservoir or bottle with airbrush paint.
2. **Dried paint accumulated in the nozzle of airbrush**. (Figure 6-3) After using your airbrush, it is important to clean the fluid nozzle thoroughly prior

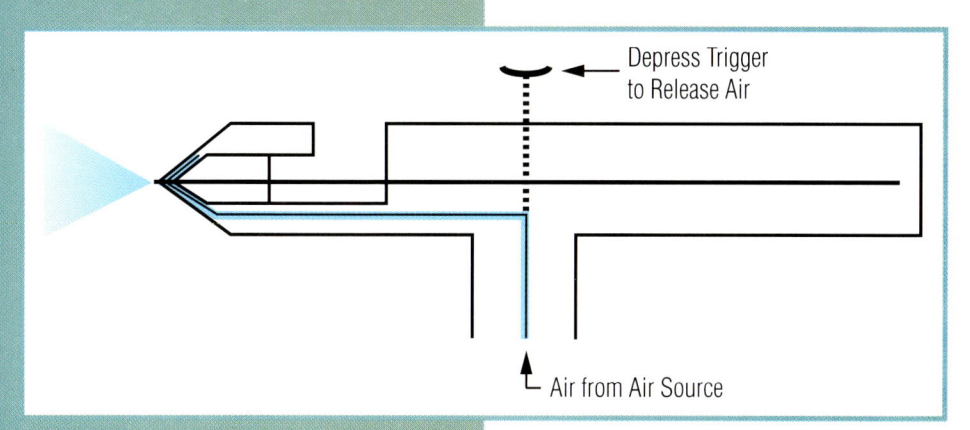

FIGURE 6-1: Pathway of air in airbrush. Air should circulate around fluid nozzle in aircap. Air creates suction which draws airbrush paint out of fluid nozzle when needle is drawn back.

77

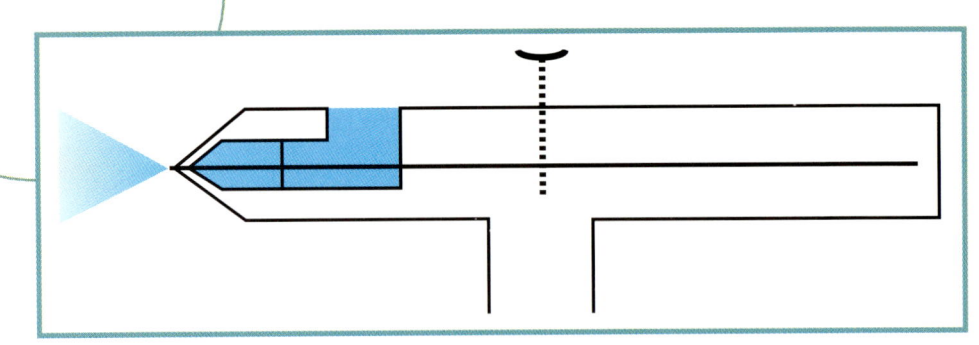

FIGURE 6-2: Pathway of paint in airbrush. Airbrush paint is located in reservoir; color cup or bottle is placed in orifice. Gravity pulls the paint into the airbrush and fluid nozzle. When the needle is drawn back, the paint should release to mix with the air and create the mist.

to storage. While using your airbrush, paint may dry on the needle blocking the airway. Use your cleaning paintbrush or toothbrush to scrub the front of the airbrush carefully to clean the dried paint away. If that doesn't solve the problem, you may need to remove the nozzle for a more thorough cleaning.

For your small fluid nozzles, as in SATA#1, DATA#1, DATA#2, soak the nozzle in airbrush cleaner for a few minutes and use the manufacturer's

CAUSE AND SOLUTION BY MODEL

Cause	SATA#1	SATA#2	DATA#1	DATA#2	DATA#3	NEWTA
No paint in color cup, reservoir or bottle	Fill cup, reservoir or bottle	Same	Same	Same	Same	Same
Dried paint in nozzle of airbrush	Soak nozzle in cleaner and use reamer or brush to remove build-up	Use pipe cleaner and acetone to scrub paint away	Soak nozzle in cleaner and use reamer or brush to remove build-up	Soak nozzle in cleaner and use reamer or brush to remove build-up	Use pipe cleaner and acetone to scrub paint away	Use brush to remove excess paint; soak nozzle
Head assembly or nozzle not attached properly	Check o-ring is in place before threading head assembly	Thread fluid nozzle onto airbrush; tighten with wrench. Thread head assembly over fluid nozzle.	Thread fluid nozzle onto airbrush; tighten with wrench. Thread head assembly over fluid nozzle.	Check o-ring is in place before threading head assembly	Hold airbrush pointing up. Place nozzle in airbrush. Thread assembly	Thread nozzle onto airbrush. Use red key to tighten.
Incorrect size nozzle for type of paint	Try fine head assembly	Only one size: .3 mm.	DOUBLE CHECK	Try fine head assembly	Sold with fine needle and nozzle	Use gray or all-purpose nozzle only

78   *Milady's Airbrushing for Nails*

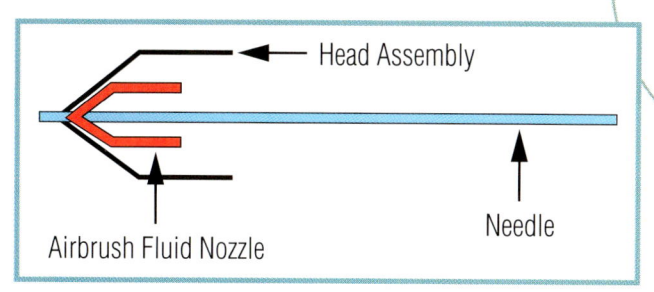

FIGURE 6-3: The airbrush fluid nozzle should fit the tapered needle precisely so that when the needle is drawn back, the paint is permitted to mix with air and is emitted from the airbrush as a mist. The airbrush fluid needle controls the release of paint. When the needle is drawn back, the airbrush paint is released along the needle. The more the needle is drawn back, the larger amount of paint is permitted down the needle. When the needle is not drawn back, it should fit the fluid nozzle precisely to prevent any paint release when the trigger is depressed for air.

reamer or brush to remove any paint build up. I do not recommend soaking the nozzles or head assemblies overnight.

For SATA#2 and DATA#3, you may use a pipe cleaner and a bit of acetone to scrub any paint accumulation away. Use the needle or manufacturer's reamer to clean the front of the nozzle.

For the NEWTA airbrushes, use a brush to remove any paint accumulation on the front of the nozzle. Place the nozzle(s) into airbrush cleaner to soak. If it is a sealed jar, you may leave the nozzles in airbrush cleaner until next use.

3. **Head assembly or nozzle is not attached properly**. Most airbrushes will not spray if the fluid nozzle has not been attached to the airbrush properly.

For SATA#2 and DATA#1, thread the fluid nozzle onto the airbrush body finger-tight. Use your wrench to tighten the fluid nozzle a one-hour turn on a clock, clockwise to seal from air leaks. Thread the head assembly over the fluid nozzle finger-tight.

For SATA#1 and DATA#2, check that the white o-ring is in place prior to threading the head assembly on the airbrush. Thread the head assembly onto the airbrush finger-tight. Use your wrench to tighten the head assembly a two-hour turn on a clock, clockwise to prevent air leaks.

For DATA#3, hold the airbrush pointing up. Place the fluid nozzle in the airbrush. Thread the head assembly onto the airbrush finger-tight. Use your wrench to tighten the head assembly a two-hour turn on the clock, clockwise.

For NEWTA, thread the nozzle onto the airbrush finger-tight. Use the red key to tighten the nozzle a one-hour-turn on the clock, clockwise.

4. **Incorrect size nozzle for type of paint**. Some airbrushes have different size nozzles available depending on the type of paint medium being used. Use the size nozzle for waterbased acrylic paints. Nozzles designed for inks or watercolors will easily clog when using acrylic mediums.

   The SATA#1 and DATA#2 are usually sold with a fine head assembly. I recommend trying the medium head assembly with a fine or medium needle if you are having problems with the airbrush clogging.

   The SATA#2 has only one size fluid nozzle, a .3mm, available. It is the correct size nozzle for airbrush nail paints.

   The DATA#1 is sold standard with a .2 mm nozzle, although there is one manufacturer selling a nail model with a .3mm nozzle. Check the literature accompanying your airbrush for the size of your fluid nozzle. This airbrush is going to clog with acrylic paints; if you can't size up your nozzle, you may have to thin your paints with distilled water. If you desire, you may use a .3 mm needle and .3 mm nozzle with this airbrush, but you must change your head assembly to the .3mm size to accommodate the larger needle.

   The DATA#3 is sold with a fine needle and nozzle that are the proper size for airbrush nail paints.

   The NEWTA is sold with a gray or all-purpose nozzle. This is the proper size nozzle for airbrush nail paints. Do not try to use the tan or fine-line nozzle since it is designed for inks and watercolors. There is a pink or spatter nozzle available which works well with airbrush nail paints for special effects.

5. **Paint has large particles in it which lodge in airbrush nozzle when spraying**. When your paint bottles set on the shelf, paint dries in the upper part of the bottle and in the dropper top. When you shake up your paint, these small fragments break away from the bottle surface and re-mix with the paint. These small chunks of dried paint are then dispensed into the airbrush when you put paint in it. To prevent this from happening, stretch a piece of nylon pantihose over the open bottle. Push or thread the dropper cap back onto the bottle. Now, every time you dispense paint, the paint will be sifted by the nylon. Eventually the nylon will become plugged with paint particles and the piece should be discarded. Place a new piece of nylon in its place.

6. **If needle is not tightened in the needle chuck, it will not permit paint to escape**. Check that needle is **seated** properly into the front of the airbrush. Push the needle forward with your fingers only; do not use tools. Tighten the needle chuck or needle knob onto the needle. Check that the needle moves back when the needle knob is turned or the trigger is pulled back.

Problem

Airbrush paint bubbles in color cup or reservoir; airbrush paint leaks from the head assembly or paint spatters from the airbrush.

POSSIBLE CAUSE AND SOLUTION

Whenever paint bubbles backward or the nozzle spatters large droplets of paint, this indicates something is wrong in the head assembly.

First, clean the front of the airbrush with a paintbrush or toothbrush to remove any dried paint that may be preventing air flow out the airbrush.

Second, make sure that the head assembly and/or nozzles are attached correctly. A loose aircap or nozzle will create these type of problems. Review previous answer number three.

If everything up front is clean, properly attached and wrench-tightened correctly, the most likely cause of your problem is a cracked or damaged fluid nozzle. Replace the fluid nozzle with your spare (the damage sometimes is difficult to see with the human eye). If the problem disappears, discard the old nozzle since it is the source of your problem.

Problem

Airbrush spits occasional droplets or needle is visibly bent. Airbrush spray emitted at an angle.

POSSIBLE CAUSE AND SOLUTION

Whenever a needle is bent, paint may accumulate in the bend and drip off the airbrush in large droplets. Be careful when cleaning the front of your airbrush not to damage the needle with your brush. Use only the bristles; never make contact with the hard part of the brush.

With traditional metal airbrushes, examine the needle prior to removing.

- If the needle is severely bent, *do not pull the needle out from the back of the airbrush!* Loosen the needle chuck or knob. Remove the head assembly and fluid nozzle carefully to avoid damage. Pull the needle out the front of the airbrush. Replace the needle.

- If the needle is slightly bent, loosen the needle chuck or knob. Pull the needle from the airbrush. Try rolling the airbrush on a hard surface at the angle of the needle bevel to straighten out the bend. You may use a fine nail file to buff away any burrs left behind. This repair works well, but each time you do it, you lose some length in the needle and the spray will be affected. Replace the needle if the bend is not reparable or if the spray has been severely affected by many repairs.

New Technology Airbrushes [NEWTA] have a needle and nozzle which are encased in a plastic head assembly. If the needle extending out the nozzle is visibly damaged (hard to do unless you have dropped the airbrush on the nozzle) replace the nozzle with your spare.

Problem

Airbrush cleaner bubbles around the head assembly.

POSSIBLE CAUSE AND SOLUTION

Airbrush paint cleaner often may bubble around the head assembly. The cleaner is as thin as water and easily seeps out the cracks in the head assembly. But when airbrush paint bubbles or seeps out it is cause for worry. If this happens, follow the directions in the preceding problem.

Problem

Airbrush spatters paint when trigger is first depressed.

POSSIBLE CAUSE AND SOLUTION

If you stop airflow before needle has been reseated in the nozzle, paint may seep in and collect in the nozzle or needle cap. When you start spraying again, this paint will spatter out prior to the regular mist. Be sure to bring the needle all the way forward before releasing your downward pressure on dual-action airbrushes. On single-action airbrushes, be sure to completely depress the trigger and release it. Pressing it half way down and then releasing will cause paint to accumulate in the needle cap of single-action airbrushes.

Problem

Needle is stuck in airbrush with dried airbrush paint.

POSSIBLE CAUSE AND SOLUTION

Loosen the needle chuck or knob. Try to wet the dried paint with airbrush paint cleaner in the airbrush. Try to rotate needle. Remove airbrush paint cleaner. Remove head assembly and fluid nozzle. Using a pair of pliers pull the needle out of the airbrush from the front. This will avoid depositing paint in the airbrush body. Clean the needle and the airbrush body thoroughly. Never drip liquids into the airbrush when the needle has been removed. Use solvent on a pipe cleaner or paintbrush to clean the paint buildup. The paint will have dried and possibly have damaged your o-ring. I recommend lubricating the o-ring with lubricant on the needle when it is replaced. Replace the parts when the airbrush is clean.

Problem

The trigger sticks or remains depressed after removing your finger pressure.

POSSIBLE CAUSE AND SOLUTION

The trigger requires lubrication. Retract the needle and remove the trigger. Wipe clean. Apply a dab of lubricant or grease to the end of the trigger. Replace the trigger. Push up and down a few times to work in the lubricant.

Problem

Airbrush trigger fails to return after being pulled back.

POSSIBLE CAUSE AND SOLUTION

With traditional dual-action metal airbrushes, the needle spring may have stuck or lost its tension. Remove handle on airbrush and twist the needle tube tension to loosen and re-tighten the tension. If this does not solve the problem, the lever assembly may have seized and require service from the manufacturer.

On a NEWTA#2, the roller on the rear of the airbrush may need to be adjusted. If the trigger fails to regain tension, it may need to be returned to the manufacturer for repair.

Problem

No air flow through airbrush.

POSSIBLE CAUSE AND SOLUTION

Remove the airbrush from the hose. If air is escaping from the hose, the problem is within your airbrush. If there is no air or inadequate pressure from the hose, there is a problem with the fittings at the moisture trap or something is wrong with the compressor.

Airbrush: Your air valve may be blocked damaged or broken. If you can find something blocking the valve on the exterior, clean it or remove it. If this does not solve the problem, some models have replacement air valves available. If you can't replace the air valve or replacing it fails to solve the problem, send the airbrush back to the manufacturer for service.

Moisture trap: If you have a threaded drain valve on your moisture trap, check that it is closed. Check the fittings attached to the moisture trap for improper fittings or need for tightening. Teflon tape should be applied to the threads of metal fittings that are going to be threaded together.

Compressor: If your compressor is not working, call manufacturer for repair assistance. You may have to return the unit for service.

CO_2 Tank: If you have no pressure from the tank when the valve is open, the tank is empty and must be replaced.

Problem

After threading the nozzle on the NEWTA #2 airbrush, the airbrush does not work properly.

POSSIBLE CAUSE AND SOLUTION

Check that the actuator is to the "+" side of the airbrush when installing the fluid nozzle. If it isn't, the nozzle may be punctured by the plunger pin and prevent the nozzle from operating properly. Remove the nozzle and move the actuator to the "+" side before reinstalling.

Problem

Coarse or spotted spray instead of desired mist from airbrush.

POSSIBLE CAUSE AND SOLUTION

1. Check your air pressure. If the pressure is too low, the paint will not atomize correctly.
2. Your paint consistency may be too thick. Add distilled water a couple drops at a time to the paint.
3. If you are using a dual-action airbrush, you must push down on the trigger while simultaneously pulling back to release paint. Many beginners tend to pull back without pushing down enough which results in a coarse spray.
4. Check the needle and fluid nozzle for damage. If you can't tell, replace the suspected part. If it solves your problem, you know the part was defective.

Problem

Air pressure seems to pulsate or is irregular.

POSSIBLE CAUSE AND SOLUTION

Check that your compressor is operating correctly. Check the electrical supply. If you have an automatic shut-off type compressor, they tend to shoot out a high pressure when the airbrush trigger is first depressed. Then the pressure may fade and surge. If this is the problem, contact the manufacturer regarding your options. They may service the unit, or you may adjust it so it stays on continuously. Use a power strip as an on and off switch.

Problem

When applying the airbrush paint bonder, the paint appears to crack or have an alligator appearance.

POSSIBLE CAUSE AND SOLUTION

Certain airbrush paints do not react well with nail polish. Test different brands to find which work best for you.

If you apply the airbrush paint so it is shiny, there may be moisture still trapped in the paint. When the nail polish contacts the water trapped in the paint, it causes the cracking or alligator appearance.

Problem

When applying the airbrush paint bonder, the paint drags with the polish brush creating lines in the airbrushed nail color.

POSSIBLE CAUSE AND SOLUTION

When applying the airbrush paint bonder you must keep the brush parallel to the nail. Be sure to have plenty of liquid on the brush; guide the liquid down the nail with the brush.

If you are moving the polish brush from an area on the nail with no paint to an area that is painted, you are more likely to move the paint with the brush.

SOME COMMON PROBLEMS

Problem	Check	What to Do
Paint bubbles in cup or reservoir	Head Assembly	Clean assembly, then check attachment is correct
Droplets; spray emitted at angle	Needle	Make sure it's not bent
Airbrush cleaner bubbles around head assembly	Nozzle or needle cap for extra cleaner	Be sure to bring needle all the way forward before releasing downward on dual-action airbrushes. On single-action airbrushes, depress trigger completely and release.
Airbrush spatters when trigger first depressed	Nozzle or needle cap for extra paint	See above.
Needle stuck in airbrush with dried paint	Needle chuck or knob.	Wet dried paint with airbrush paint cleaner. Try rotating needle. Clean needle and airbrush and body. Lubricate o-ring.

Airbrushing Basics

Chapter 7

Introduction and Marketing of Airbrush Nail Services

Introduction

People have been airbrushing nails for over twenty years. Why then has it not become a fundamental part of the nail technician's training and income? Most people think airbrushing is an art form and that it is an accessory to nail services. My approach to airbrushing nails has been different, and as a result, has made me more money. Would you like to make more money? Most people I know would!

Years ago I worked with Robert Sanders, an airbrush artist and at the time a manufacturer in California. He introduced me to the concept of applying all nail color with an airbrush. At first, this idea seemed radical, but with a few modifications to his methods and ideas, I started sharing this concept with other nail technicians. As nail technicians, we have been indoctrinated to apply traditional nail polish. It is an accepted part of the nail service. If a client comes in for her nail service and is running behind schedule, she may request no polish. Does the price change for the service if the client does not receive traditional nail polish? Most of us would say no. Whether the client has nail polish, the price remains the same. You actually earn your money doing the nail service; *while you are applying nail polish no revenue is generated!*

If you compare our nail industry to the hair industry, you will see many similarities. Fifteen years ago, if you asked a salon how much it would cost for a hair cut, they would reply one price. This price would include the shampoo, haircut, drying and styling of the hair. If you ask the same question today, you will receive an entirely different answer. Most salons would quote a price for the haircut, a separate price for the shampoo/conditioning and another price for the drying and styling. Today, most hair salons fall into two categories: a salon full of progressive, knowledgeable staff of hair designers or an old fashioned "roller-cranker" salon. The nail industry is headed for the same type of division.

What happened to the income of the "beautician" who took the time to become educated in current trends in hair design and chemical services? Both the status, the title and the income changed—they became higher! Most hair designers will correct you if you call them a "beautician" or "beauty operator." They prefer to be called a hair designer, hair artist or beauty consultant. Many cosmetologists are proud of what they do and want a title and income to match their skills. The status of hair professionals is perceived as higher today, compared to how they were recognized fifteen years ago. When the hair stylist began charging for every service they completed on a client, their income naturally increased. They were being paid for every minute they spent with their client. We need to look at our work schedule and be able to charge for every minute we spend servicing a nail client.

I still meet nail technicians who mumble under their breath when asked their occupation. It is time to earn the income and respect that you deserve (and want)! The first step is to raise your feelings of self worth. One of the best ways I know to make you feel more confident is to increase your business and technical knowledge. Learn everything you can about nails and marketing, and be the best that you can be. The next step is to increase your income. Airbrushing will do that! I foresee the same division occurring in nail salons that we have seen in hair salons. There will be progressive nail and beauty salons offering professional airbrush nail color as well as salons that offer only traditional nail polish. I am already aware of nail color technicians who specialize exclusively in airbrushed nail color applications. When you offer your clients a choice in nail color applications, it will distinguish your nail services from others in your area.

I introduced every new technique I could to my clients. Airbrushing nail color was by far the most profitable service. It was obvious by the number of clients who took advantage of it, but it was most noticeable in the increase in income! Think about it! At this time you are donating time to your client by applying nail polish. If you do eight clients a day and take ten minutes to apply polish, that adds up to eighty minutes a day that you are working for free! That is 400 minutes or more than six and a half hours for which you are not paid. *That means at this time you are working for five days and get paid for only four days and one hour.* Think if you could generate some money during that "free" time.

In order to offer airbrushed nail services, you must be ready to airbrush at your nail table or pedicure station at any time. If you are set up and ready, the actual service of applying airbrushed nail color takes only minutes. Nail technicians tend to get intimidated by some of the initial difficulties they encounter when learning to airbrush. When you first learned to apply a set of nails, did you apply them as well or as quickly as you do today? Of course not. Anything worthwhile will take practice to master the skill. Once you know how to do something, it is easier to accomplish and takes much less time.

It is the same with airbrushing. When you are learning, it will be slow. Once you have mastered it, you will be able to apply a simple color fade or traditional French manicure in the same amount of time it took to apply traditional nail polish. The client gets something special and you get to charge a small fee for the upgrade in service. If you add three to five dollars to each client's service, that would increase your income $24 to $40 a day without increasing your work hours! Would you like to add $10,000 to your gross annual income? That's what will happen if you offer your clients a choice in nail color application. I am not even calculating the additional money you will earn applying airbrushed nail art! That $10,000 is a significant increase to your income without costing you more time!

I did a lot of designs that required hand-cut nail masks. I would cut the nail masks before work, during cancellations or at home while watching TV. I usually had a whole side of a glass plate full of Chevron French manicure nail masks and striping nail masks ready. If it's ready, it takes no time to apply and spray. During the holidays, I had my holiday designs cut out in triplicate, in case someone had a last minute request (and I had the time in my schedule).

Airbrush Nail Services: The Give-Away!

It is very easy to get your clients interested in airbrushed nails instead of applying traditional nail polish. While you are practicing on nail tips, save the nails that you like and display them for clients to see. I recommend having two displays. One display should have only conservative looks. Some clients are scared of airbrushed nails because they immediately think of wild patterns and pictures they have seen. Show them soft color fades with subtle changes, bolder color fades, traditional French manicures, Chevron French manicures and other fancy French manicures. I guarantee there will be something your client wants to try before her service is over.

The other display may contain your airbrushed nail art. Keep this display out of sight from the conservative client until she is educated about airbrushing and has worn it. Then show off your artwork to that client. You never know! Many conservative clients love nail art on their toes; over vacation she may wear something different or, she might have a friend who loves to go all out. Stress to your clients that they may wear two or three favorite nail colors at the same time. This helps with wardrobe changes. If they are wearing coral, pink and red they have most clothing color combinations covered. Airbrushed nail color offers the client more choices than traditional nail polish ever could.

When first introducing the option of airbrushed nail color to your clients, offer the service free for the first time only. Let them wear home a color fade or airbrushed French manicure. The airbrushed French manicure has no bumps, thickness and dries quickly. It is a big improvement over traditional polish. Always tell them how much the airbrushing would cost if they want it again. You must qualify the value of your giveaway in order to charge next time. They will go home, go shopping, go to work and people will rave about their nails. Even if it is a very subtle color change, they will feel special. Airbrushed nail color makes a statement. It says "These nails were professionally done" without your client saying a word. In short, airbrushing is addictive, just like the nail service itself. Many women don't look in a mirror all day, but they look at their hands all the time. If their hands and nails are attractive, they feel good. They will continue having their nails done and airbrushed because it makes them feel special. For many women this is the only time they take for themselves.

The Price List

The best marketing tool in a salon is a price list or menu listing of the services you offer. Many times you will hear a client exclaim they didn't realize you offered "such and such" service. A price list also acts as a clear agreement or contract with your client. When a client reviews your price list and requests a service, the client is aware of the cost. This avoids unnecessary confusion and possible haggling when the time to pay the bill arrives. A price list provides an equal system of billing clients, even for those clients who think they are special and deserve different.

Price your airbrushing competitively. You may wish to offer an introductory price to interest new business in your airbrush nail services. For your regular clients, offer the "first time free" deal and then go to your regular pricing. Your pricing on any service should reflect your expertise. As with anything, the client gets what she pays for. So when you first start airbrushing, you will not be able to charge as much as someone who has been airbrushing for two years; that person may not be able to charge the same price as a veteran of ten years. Again, the better your skills and quality of product, the more money you will make. This should be true of any profession, though I find many people who do not realize their value in the nail industry.

There are many discount nail salons opening across the country. I will use the hair industry as an example again. The hair industry has had discount salons for years now. But do you see hair designers upscale salons charging twice—possibly three times—the price of a discount salon going out of business? If they are skilled, conscientious hair designers, they are as busy as ever. Don't lower your prices in fear of discount salons. There are all different types of clients in your area. There are people who desire quality products with expert service who are willing to pay for it. The key here is that you are knowledgeable and ethical. In other words, the best you can be. There are other clients who cannot afford the upscale salon. They would never have had their nails professionally done if the lower priced salons did not open. There is plenty of business for every type of nail business, whether you are promoting expertise, quality of products, speed of service or low price.

Most people include their nail polish application in the price of their nail services. Once you start offering airbrushed nail color as an alternative, your clients have greater choice in nail color. If you offer one color of traditional nail polish in

SAMPLE PRICE LIST

NAIL SERVICE	PRICE
SET OF ARTIFICIAL NAILS	$55.00
ARTIFICIAL NAIL MAINTENANCE	25.00
MANICURE	15.00
PEDICURE	30.00
NAIL COLOR APPLICATION: One airbrush nail color or polish included with any of the above services.	
SECOND AIRBRUSH COLOR	5.00
THIRD AND EACH ADDITIONAL AIRBRUSH COLOR	3.00
FRENCH MANICURE, NATURAL CURVE	5.00
FRENCH MANICURE, NATURAL CURVE, LUNULA/MOON AT CUTICLE	8.00
FRENCH MANICURE, CHEVRON	15.00
FRENCH MANICURE, CHEVRON WITH A CHEVRON MOON	18.00
AIRBRUSHED NAIL ART	*See Design Board

Masks or stencil nail designs are priced according to amount of time it takes to create the design.

*ANY AIRBRUSH NAIL COLOR FADE COMBINATION UP TO THREE COLORS OR A TRADITIONAL FRENCH MANICURE MAY BE APPLIED DURING SCHEDULED SERVICE WITH TIME ALLOTTED FOR COLOR. ARTISTIC OR GRAPHIC COMBINATIONS MUST BE BOOKED IN ADVANCE SINCE THEY REQUIRE MORE TIME.

the price, your price now to be fair, would include the choice of an airbrushed nail color. That is why it is important to give them a multiple airbrushed nail color for free one time. Once someone has worn a color fade, it is very difficult to go back to wearing one solid nail color.

After you have mastered airbrushing nail color, you should be able to accomplish a two, three or four color fade and traditional French manicure in the time it took to apply traditional nail polish. If the client desires some airbrushed nail art, stenciled designs are usually easy to add in without much additional time. For any other airbrushed nail art, additional time must be booked in advance. Have this clearly stipulated on your price list so a client won't be disappointed. When special events come up, they will know to book in advance the airbrushed nail art they want…which offers you some time to prepare.

The sample price list is strictly to give you an idea of how to outline your pricing for customers. Prices may need to be adjusted higher or lower for your area and according to your expertise. Many nail technicians employ a per color and per design tool type of pricing scale. I charge per color for color fades and French manicures. If you time yourself and set a price for each design it is easier (and more fair) for the client to understand. Most airbrush nail color technicians feel that one dollar per minute airbrushing is a fair price. Again, you must make the final decision on what is a fair price for your business.

Business Building Strategies

Have you noticed that your clients tend to want the nail color you are wearing? I used to change my nail color often since I would always run out of the polish I was wearing. Well the same is true for airbrushed nail color. You must wear airbrushed nail color and so should your co-workers in order to promote this addictive service. If the clients always want what you are wearing, that should tell you not to wear the least expensive application. Wear a three- or four-color design that will cost the client five or ten dollars extra. If you have a predominantly conservative clientele I recommend *not* wearing airbrushed nail art on all ten nails for the first six months since it may intimidate them from having their nails airbrushed. I usually wear a soft three- or four-color blend with nail art on one or two of my fingers.

Go shopping at a mall or strip center in your area. Every time I shop, when I sign my check or charge slip, the retail clerks practically jump over the counter to have a closer look at my nails. They find it unbelievable that the color can change from light to dark or that my French manicure looks so natural. They always ask where I had my nails done. People in retail have their hands and nails on display all day. They are perfect advertisements for your work. Offer them a discount if you have to, to get them into your salon. If you can't wear your airbrushing, be sure to shop with someone who does wear your work. Always carry business cards in your pocket to give people you meet while shopping. I had a rubber stamp which printed "five dollars off your first visit" on my business card. My business card was a coupon.

Use the surrounding businesses to promote your airbrushed nail services. Try to frequent your neighbors for business and they will return the favor. Ask if they would mind if you left business cards, price lists or your current flyer on their counter. Many people will be happy to help out, especially if they are one of your customers.

Don't forget to ask your existing clientele to help you build your business. If a client is referred to you or requests you after seeing your work, they are a sure new addition to your clientele. Ask your clients if they mind distributing your business card or current flyer at their business, with friends and family. Many offices have bulletin boards where you can display a poster, a press release or a flyer. Attach a pocket for your business cards or coupons. Many clients won't think about recommending you. Ask them to. Give them a few business cards and ask them to hand them out. If a client brings you a new client, I immediately reward them with a free airbrushing or manicure after the new client has been serviced. If they realize they can get something free for sending you new business, they will be more effective sales people for you.

CUSTOM-BLENDED NAIL COLOR

One of the best-selling features of working with airbrush paint is that it is so easy to mix the paint to create new colors. All of us know how often clients bring a swatch of fabric to the salon for a special occasion. Now instead of finding only a color that is close to the fabric, how about offering the client the chance to match it. It takes time to color match and mix a new color. After you have mixed a dozen custom paint colors (technique described in COLOR THEORY Chapter), your mixing time will be greatly reduced. As with anything, a little practice speeds up the process the next time. Most airbrushed nail color technicians charge a small fee for the time it will take to match the color. You may also wish to pick or blend additional airbrush paint colors to create a custom fade or nail art design which compliments the outfit. A wonderful effect for bridesmaids is a chevron French manicure with a stripe matching their gowns. The bride may wear a traditional chevron French manicure or also wear the stripe.

Every year many traditional nail polish manufacturers discontinue nail polish colors that clients love. Now these clients have somewhere to go to continue getting their favorite nail color. To you. Many airbrush nail color technicians mix airbrush nail paints of their most popular nail polish colors. When their polish testers run out, they don't replace them. It saves the salon money and offers a professional nail color service to the client. You will maintain, if not increase your retail sales, since the client will purchase protective glaze to maintain their nails (and your guarantee) and a nail polish that matches their nail tip color for home touch-ups if necessary. After the nail service, only professional airbrushed nail color is applied. If the client insists on traditional nail polish, they must supply or purchase a bottle from the salon to use.

Conclusion

Airbrush nail services offers the professional nail technician an income potential never achieved before. By adding airbrush nail services beyond just nail art, you will recoup your initial investment in airbrush equipment, supplies and education in a few months. If it was just for nail art it would take much longer to break even and get ahead.

WAYS TO MARKET YOUR NEW AIRBRUSHING SERVICE

1. Give away a free first-time airbrushing.
2. Create displays of airbrushed nail tips, one a conservative set, the other with more creative nail art.
3. Wear your work—and encourage others in the salon to do the same.
4. Post a price list or menu of services.
5. Enlist surrounding businesses to help display your flyers, cards or price lists.
6. Ask clients for referrals.

If you follow the marketing strategies in this book, most nail technicians will significantly increase their income without increasing their hours. For those of you who are overworked and stressed out, this means a way to reduce your work hours to a reasonable schedule.

For everyone, airbrush nail services offers the nail technician the ability to experience the joy of doing nails professionally. There is nothing that compares to that feeling of pride when your customer admires the miracle you have accomplished on their hands or feet. Most professional nail technicians started out doing nails because they loved working on nails. Over the years many of us have been working too hard and have forgotten the fun of doing nails. I hope airbrushing nail color and nail art will bring back the joy of nail technology to you as it did for me. Good luck, practice hard and stop by when you see me at a show and say hello!

Part 2
Airbrushing Technicals

Each of the following 14 technicals begins with a list of necessary supplies. Keep in mind that you can vary the suggested colors — experiment with different blends! If, however, you want your designs to look like those in this book, use the colors as listed in the supplies section for each technical.

Technical 1: Solid Nail Color

The solid nail color technique is employed when the client wants one nail color or as the first step of an airbrushed nail color service.

Supplies

Base coat; crystalline, special effect or white, as needed
Airbrush cleaner
Mauve airbrush paint
Nail bonder
Protective glaze

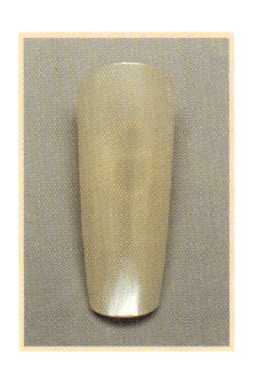

STEP 1

Apply your base coat to the nail. If the nail has a dark tone or you are using a transparent airbrush nail paint, apply a crystalline, special effect or white base coat.

Airbrushing Technicals 97

STEP 2

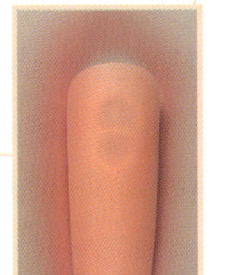

Place a couple drops of airbrush cleaner into your airbrush. Spray out all of the airbrush cleaner into your cleaning station or cleaning receptacle. Place your airbrush paint color into your airbrush. Always start your paint feeding into your airbrush by spraying onto the surface next to your nails. I have chosen mauve as my color. When the airbrush paint is loaded into your airbrush and is spraying correctly, you are ready to begin application on the nail. Apply a dry, even coat by going up and down the nail, moving your whole arm. If you are working on more than one nail, apply this light, dry coat to all the nails.

STEP 3

Continue applying light, dry coats of airbrush paint until you have reached the desired color or opacity on the nail. After you have completed all nails, apply your nail paint bonder and let it dry for three minutes. If you are not going to continue airbrushing, clean up your airbrush at this time. Apply the protective glaze for durability. Instruct your client on home maintenance of the airbrushed nail color.

STEP 4

The completed solid color nail looks very much like a traditional nail polish at first glance. However, upon closer observation, you will see it is a much thinner coating on the nail. The pigment, if applied correctly, will be even with no irregularities and the coating will appear smooth with no brushstrokes. In the photo, the left nail tip is coral, the center nail tip is mauve and the nail tip on the right is red solid airbrushed nail color.

Technical 2: Nail Color Contour

The nail color contour technique will be employed when the client wants her nails to appear narrower or longer. The completed nail will have the look of a solid-color nail, but upon closer examination, one may see that the color on the sides are slightly darker than the color down the center. This technique creates an illusion of a thinner or longer nail for your client, similar to contouring the face with makeup. It is a two-color airbrush nail service which justifies an additional charge for the nail color application. This technique may be used as the background for an airbrushed nail design or on its own as an airbrushed nail color service for a conservative client.

Supplies

BASE COAT; CRYSTALLINE, SPECIAL EFFECT OR WHITE, AS NEEDED
AIRBRUSH CLEANER
CLEANING STATION
CORAL AIRBRUSH PAINT
RED-ORANGE AIRBRUSH PAINT
NAIL PAINT BONDER
PROTECTIVE GLAZE

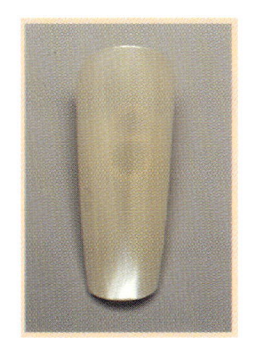

STEP 1

Apply your base coat to the nail.

Airbrushing Technicals

STEP 2

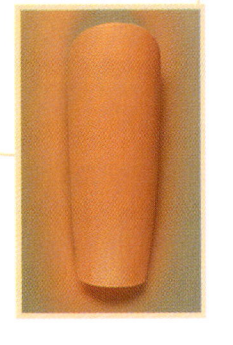

Place a couple drops of airbrush cleaner into your airbrush. Spray out all of the airbrush cleaner into your cleaning station or cleaning receptacle. Place your airbrush paint color into your airbrush. Always start your paint feeding into your airbrush by spraying onto the surface next to your nails. I have chosen coral as my color. When the airbrush paint is loaded into your airbrush and is spraying correctly, you are ready to begin application. Apply a dry, even coat by going up and down the nail, moving your whole arm. If you are working on more than one nail, apply this light, dry coat to all the nails. Continue applying light, dry coats of airbrush paint until you have reached the desired color or opacity on the nail.

STEP 3

Clean your airbrush of the first paint. Choose a color that is darker than the first. The closer the colors are in hue, the more subtle the shading. I have chosen red-orange for a more visible contour of the nail sides. When airbrushing the second color, aim for each side of the nail. Move your arm up and down to lightly spray each side of the nails. Repeat the procedure until you have achieved the desired color on each side. If you are getting color in the middle of the nail, try aiming at the surface (the finger, board, nail table or your hand) directly next to the nail.

STEP 4

After you have completed all nails, apply your nail paint bonder and let it dry for three minutes. If you are not going to continue airbrushing, clean up your airbrush at this time. Apply the airbrush paint protective glaze for durability. Instruct your client on home maintenance of the airbrushed nail color.

STEP 5

The first nail in the photo is bubblegum pink, with magenta as the contour color. The second nail is the coral, contoured with red-orange nail tip. The nail on the right is a red nail, color contoured with dark red.

Technical 3:

TWO-COLOR FADE
(COLOR BLEND)

The nail color fade or color blend is one of the most popular airbrush nail color services. The color fade may work for a conservative client when subtle, soft hues of similar colors are used. Or, it may be a bold color fade for the outgoing client when colors strongly contrast. This service will appeal to every client. The colors are key to the success of this design. It is a multi-color airbrush nail service which justifies an additional charge for the nail color application. This technique may be used as the background for an airbrushed nail design or on its own as an airbrushed nail color service.

Supplies

BASE COAT; CRYSTALLINE, SPECIAL EFFECT OR WHITE, AS NEEDED
AIRBRUSH CLEANER
CLEANING STATION
MAGENTA PEARL AIRBRUSH PAINT
TURQUOISE PEARL
NAIL PAINT BONDER
PROTECTIVE GLAZE

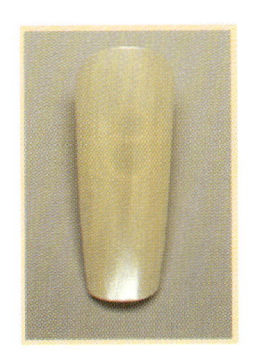

STEP 1

Apply your base coat to the nail.

Airbrushing Technicals — 101

STEP 2

Place a couple drops of airbrush cleaner into your airbrush. Spray out all of the airbrush cleaner into your cleaning station or cleaning receptacle. Place your airbrush paint color into your airbrush. Always start your paint feeding into your airbrush by spraying onto the surface next to your nails. I have chosen a magenta pearl as my first color. When the airbrush paint is loaded into your airbrush and spraying correctly, you are ready to begin application.

TIP *When using pearlescent paints, the airbrush may clog easier. I suggest that you use pearlescent airbrush paints only after you have mastered your opaque and transparent paints!*

Apply a dry, even coat going back and forth diagonally over the top two-thirds of the nail, moving your whole arm. If you are working on more than one nail, apply this light, dry coat diagonally to all the nails.

TIP *With the pearlescent paint, you may have to pull your hand further away from the nail and release slightly more paint to get an even spray. Practice will make the adjustment smoother. Apply more coats of the airbrush paint at the cuticle area, with fewer coats toward the center of the nail to create a soft edge for the second color to overlap.*

STEP 3

Continue applying light, dry coats of airbrush paint diagonally until you have reached the desired color or opacity in the nail cuticle area fading towards the center.

STEP 4

Clean your airbrush of the first color. Choose a color that is appropriate for your client. I have chosen a turquoise pearl paint to contrast and create a transition color with my magenta pearl. When airbrushing the second color, start at the bottom of the nail tip and move up two thirds of the nail. Apply more coats over the free edge or nail tip, with fewer coats through the center of the nail. If the colors mix when overlapped, you will begin to see the transition color (violet in this case) start to develop.

102   Milady's Airbrushing for Nails

STEP 5

Continue to apply a dry, even coat going back and forth diagonally over the bottom two-thirds of the nail, until you have achieved the desired color at the free edge of the nail. If a transition color does develop, you control the color by the amount of overlap. Remember when working on your client, the airbrushed color fade on the right hand should be a mirror image of the color fade on the left hand. I prefer to have the colors travel from the outer corner of the nail (towards the pinkie finger) towards the inner corner of the cuticle (towards the thumb). But each airbrush artist has her own preference.

STEP 6

After you have completed all nails, apply your nail paint bonder and let it dry for three minutes. If you are not going to continue airbrushing, cleanup your airbrush at this time. Apply the airbrush paint protective glaze for durability. Instruct your client on home maintenance of the airbrushed nail color.

The photo shows a few possible variations of this design. The nail tip on the left is a subtle blend for the conservative client. It is a cognac nail color with a transparent gold shimmer splashed at the free edge. The center nail is a bit more daring; pearl red in the cuticle fading into a true pink nail tip. The nail tip on the right in the photo is the nail tip completed in our step-by-step directions above. This nail color selection is for your bold client who wants people to notice her nails!

Airbrushing Technicals

ID# Technical 4:

MULTIPLE COLOR FADE

From this technical on, I will list only the unique steps to the new designs. If you need a reminder on starting the operation of your airbrush, or cleaning it, please review the appropriate chapters.

This technical is very similar to technical 3, only we will discuss how to apply three or more airbrush colors to the nails. This airbrushed nail service, once you have practiced, may be accomplished in the same amount of time that you scheduled for nail polish.

Supplies

BASE COAT; CRYSTALLINE, SPECIAL EFFECT OR WHITE, AS NEEDED
AIRBRUSH CLEANER
CLEANING STATION
OPAQUE CORAL
OPAQUE TRUE PINK
BUBBLEGUM PINK
NAIL PAINT BONDER
PROTECTIVE GLAZE

STEP 1

Apply your base coat to the nail(s). Use a crystalline base coat for transparent paint or to neutralize the color of the nail plate or tip. When using opaque airbrush color, as I will in this technical, you may use a clear base coat if desired.

Milady's Airbrushing for Nails

STEP 2

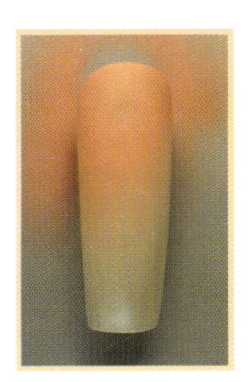

Apply the first color of your color fade. I tend to start at the cuticle area of the nail; however, you may start at the nail tip if you prefer. I have chosen opaque coral for the cuticle area. I am only going to use three colors, so each of my colors will cover one-third of the nail. If I wanted a four-color blend, each color would cover one-fourth of the nail, etc.

STEP 3

Apply your second color slightly overlapping the first, covering the center third of the nail. If you were using airbrush colors that mix, you would begin to see your first transitional color develop where the two colors overlap. I am using opaque true pink, so the colors are not mixing, simply overlapping.

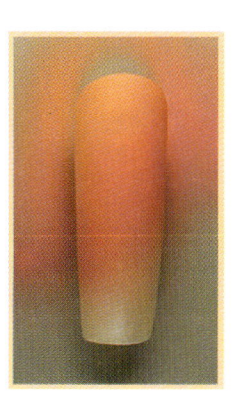

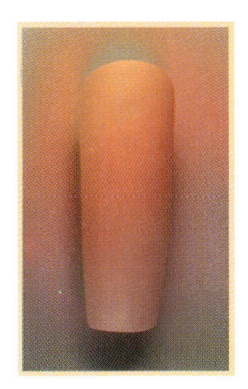

STEP 4

The third color will be applied over the final exposed third of the nail, overlapping the second color. I am using bubblegum pink as my final color. Remember when working on your client, the airbrushed color fade on the right hand should be a mirror image of the color fade on the left hand. I prefer to have the colors travel from the outer corner of the nail (near the pinkie finger) towards the inner corner of the cuticle (towards the thumb).

STEP 5

After you have completed all nails, apply your nail paint bonder and let it dry for three minutes. Apply the airbrush paint protective glaze for durability.

Airbrushing Technicals

STEP 6

The photo demonstrates how versatile the airbrush nail color fade may be. The nail on the left is a three-color fade using the three primary colors in pearlescent paint. Pearlescent colors mix slightly, as seen in technical 3. When the red and yellow overlap, we develop a transition color of orange. When the blue and yellow overlap, we develop a transition color of green. When you overlap three airbrush paints that mix, the client receives the benefit of having a five color result! Notice that the yellow, green and blue are placed towards the nail tip, avoiding contact with the skin if possible.

The center nail is our completed design from technical 4. It is a subtle blend, using a red triad (tint of red-orange or coral, tint of red or true pink, tint of red-violet or bubblegum pink). The third nail tip on the right is a four color blend using pearl white at the cuticle, pearl magenta, gold shimmer and black at the nail tip.

106 Milady's Airbrushing for Nails

Technical 5:

TRADITIONAL FRENCH MANICURE (WITH OPTIONAL LUNULA)

The French manicure is the most popular reason why most nail technicians look into airbrushed nail color. The hand-polished French manicure cannot compare to the airbrushed version. I always show my new nail technology students how to hand-polish the French, then I demonstrate the airbrushed French. The airbrushed French is easier, quicker and more attractive than the hand-polished version.

The airbrushed French manicure has a clean, sophisticated look while being a neutral color that matches all clothing. Each airbrush nail technician has their own favorite method of achieving the traditional French manicure, which is a skin toned nail bed with a curved white tip. There are three popular methods for achieving the curved nail tip, demonstrated in this technical. All three methods may add the white lunula or moon to the cuticle area if desired (for a slight additional charge!)

Supplies

BASE COAT OR FRENCH MANICURE PINK
AIRBRUSH CLEANER
CLEANING STATION
FRENCH MANICURE BEIGE
DISTILLED WATER
GOLD HIGHLIGHT OR SHIMMER (OPTIONAL)
CURVED EDGE STENCIL OR HANDCUT NAIL MASK
FOR A HAND-CUT NAIL MASK:
— SMALL PIECE OF GLASS
— MASK KNIFE
— CIRCLE OR CURVED TEMPLATE OR JAR OR GLASS FOR TRACING
WHITE NAIL TIP PAINT
NAIL PAINT BONDER
PROTECTIVE GLAZE

Airbrushing Technicals

STEP 1

Apply a clear base coat to the nail(s). You may use a French manicure polish to achieve the nail bed color if desired. Allow plenty of time for the nail polish to dry. If you choose not to airbrush the nail bed color, skip to step 4. I have used a crystalline base coat to neutralize the color of the nail tip.

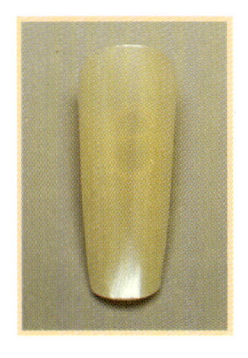

STEP 2

Choose your French manicure airbrush paint. I have chosen a French beige. Refer to the color theory chapter for suggested French manicure paint formulations. You may customize your formulations for your clients so they have "their personal color." Mist the French manicure color over the nail lightly. Continue passing your airbrush over the nail until the desired color or opacity is achieved. If your client wants a transparent French manicure color, you may mist the opaque color lightly. Most airbrush paint colors may be made slightly transparent by adding a couple drops of distilled water.

STEP 3

Optional: Add a shimmer to your French manicure paint. I have misted a gold highlight or shimmer evenly over the French beige.

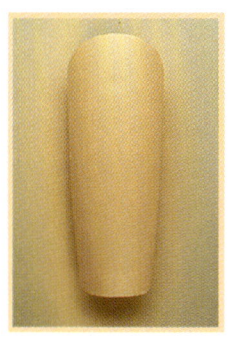

STEP 4

French tip application with a stencil: Use a curved edge to cover the nail bed color and expose the nail tip to be sprayed white. This is an excellent method for a soft-edged French nail tip.

- You may cut a curved piece of paper (same method as cutting nail mask in step #5) or use a ready-made stencil.
- Hold the stencil as closely to the nail as possible, exposing the nail tip to be sprayed. Keep the stencil parallel to the nail to avoid scratching the paint on the nail.

- When you have the stencil lined up, mist the nail tip white. Build the color slowly, to avoid getting the paint wet and runny. (Watch the edge of your stencil if it is plastic. The paint accumulates easily and may run down onto the nail. Dry the stencil with air from your airbrush without moving it. It is difficult to line the stencil precisely the same again.
- When working with stencils, I mist paint, then blow air to dry the nail tip and stencil. I repeat this process until the nail tip is the color I want.

STEP 5

French tip application with a hand-cut nail mask: There are a number of items you may use to hand-cut the nail mask for a curved French manicure. Anything hard that has the desired curve would be excellent to trace on the nail mask paper. There are or curved templates for graphic artists available. You may also trace a lid from a jar, or trace a glass placed on the mask. Some of the cutting triangles we use have a circle in them which are excellent to trace. Using French nail masks will produce a crisp-edged white tip.

- Remove the paper backing on your mask paper. (Scrunch one end of the paper between your fingers to start separating it.) Place the nail mask paper on a piece of glass. Place the item to be traced at the top of your mask paper. Trace half a circle onto the mask paper with the mask knife. Repeat the procedure until you have ten nail masks, one for each finger. I cut these nail masks ahead of time (at least a hundred at a time, so I'm ready when clients request this service.)
- Place the nail mask over each finger, protecting the nail bed color and exposing the nail tip to be sprayed. Use your finger or thumb (no nails!) to press the mask tightly to the nail. If the nail mask is not tight, paint may get under it.
- Mist the nail tip white. Build the color slowly on each nail tip, to avoid getting the paint wet and runny. If the paint becomes wet, it may bleed the color under the nail mask. When airbrushing ten nails, I work on five at a time to avoid overspraying the white and getting the paint wet. (Watch the edge of your nail mask. The paint easily accumulates and may run down onto the nail. Blow air to dry the nail mask and tip if it gets wet.) Repeat this process until the nail tip is the color desired.
- When you remove the nail masks, be sure to peel the masks back off the nail. If you pull the masks straight up off the nails, the masks may pull paint with them.

Airbrushing Technicals

STEP 6

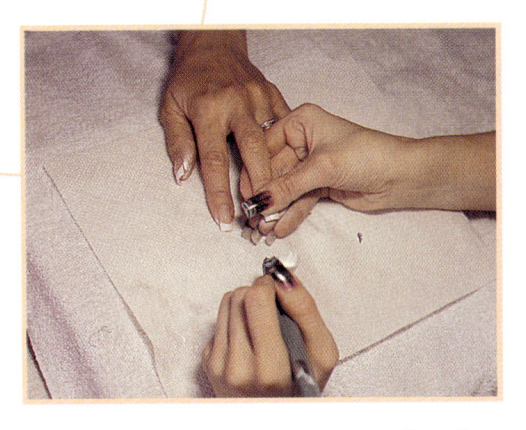

French tip application using your thumb as a stencil: Experiment pressing your thumb down on the side of the table. Find the fleshy part of your thumb that forms a curve when pressed against the table. When practicing on nail tips, place them on the edge of your board so you can place your thumb over them. Place your thumb over the nail tip as if you were holding someone's hand. After a bit of practice, this technique is excellent for creating a soft-edged French tip.

- Be sure your thumb is clean and free of oils. Place your thumb over the client's nail bed exposing the nail tip to be sprayed white. Mist your white paint, slowly building up color. If the paint starts to get wet, mist air over it. When you have achieved the desired color, remove your thumb. If your thumb wants to stick to the paint, roll your thumb off the nail to avoid pulling paint with you.

STEP 7

If the nails you are working on are very curved, you may have to touch up the stenciled nails. Using your thumb or stencil, roll the finger sideways and carefully line up your thumb/stencil with the white tip already sprayed. Mist the sides of the nail to match and complete the white tip.

STEP 8

Adding a lunula or moon with a stencil creates the "real" look. Mist the lunula slightly lighter than the nail tip color.

STEP 9

After you have completed all nails, apply your nail paint bonder and let it dry for three minutes. Apply the airbrush paint protective glaze for durability.

STEP 10

This photo shows the three French manicure techniques next to each other. The left nail tip was done with a stencil; the center nail tip was created with a nail mask; the right nail tip was created with my thumb.

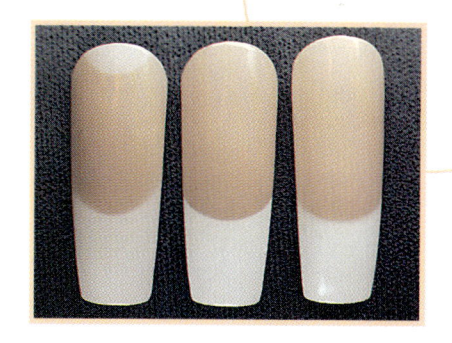

STEP 11

This procedure is easily accomplished on toes. Use your preferred method to apply a French manicure to the toes.

STEP 12

Cleanse the toes with airbrush paint cleaner after they have been bonded and glazed.

STEP 13

This photo is of our model with a traditional French manicure on her fingernails and toenails.

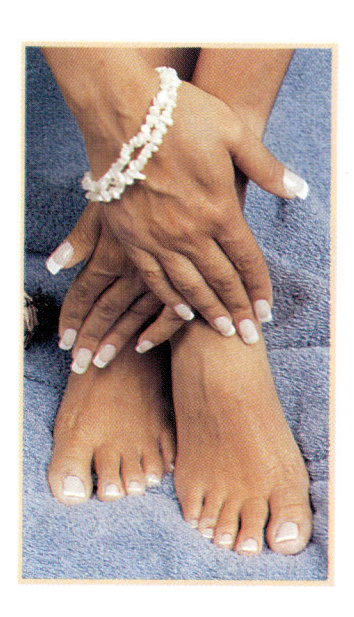

Airbrushing Technicals   *111*

Technical 6:

CHEVRON FRENCH MANICURE
(WITH OPTIONAL CHEVRON LUNULA)

The French manicure has developed many variations over the years. The chevron-shaped French white tip is easily accomplished. The following technical demonstrates two popular methods for achieving the chevron French manicure look.

Supplies

BASE COAT
AIRBRUSH CLEANER
CLEANING STATION
FRENCH MANICURE PEACH PAINT
PINK OPAL HIGHLIGHT (OPTIONAL)
CHEVRON STENCIL; PAPER OR PLASTIC OR CHEVRON STENCIL OR HAND-CUT NAIL MASK
HAND-CUT MASK SUPPLIES:
— NAIL MASK PAPER
— CUTTING TRIANGLES
— PIECE OF GLASS
— MASK KNIFE
WHITE NAIL TIP COLOR
NAIL PAINT BONDER
PROTECTIVE GLAZE

STEP 1

Apply a clear base coat to the nail(s).

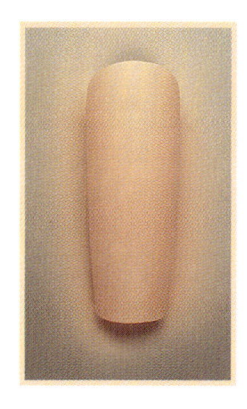

STEP 2

Choose your French manicure airbrush paint. I have chosen a French peach. Refer to the color theory chapter for suggested French manicure paint formulations. Mist the French manicure color over the nail lightly. If you desire the color to be opaque, continue passing over the nail until the desired color or opacity is achieved. If your client desires a transparent French manicure color, you may mist the opaque color lightly. Most airbrush paint colors may be made slightly transparent by adding a couple drops of distilled water.

STEP 3

Optional: Add a shimmer to your French manicure paint. I have misted a pink opal highlight or shimmer evenly over the French peach.

STEP 4

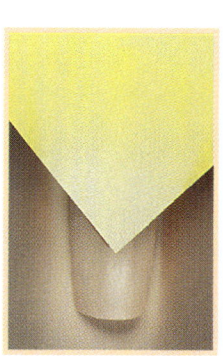

Chevron French tip application with a stencil: You will use a corner edge (90° angle) to cover the nail bed color and expose the nail tip to be sprayed white. This is an excellent method for a soft-edged Chevron French nail tip.

- You may cut a corner from a piece of paper (same method as cutting nail mask in step #5). Many people use business cards, but I find them too stiff. Also, there are many ready-made stencils on the market.
- Hold the stencil as closely to the nail as possible, exposing the nail tip to be sprayed. Keep the stencil parallel or wrapped around the nail to avoid scratching the paint on the nail.
- When you have the stencil lined up, mist the nail tip white. Build the color slowly, to avoid getting the paint wet and runny. (Watch the edge of your stencil if it is plastic. The paint accumulates easily and may run down onto the nail. Dry the stencil with air from your airbrush without moving it. It is difficult to line the stencil precisely the same again.)
- When working with stencils, I tend to mist paint then blow air to dry the nail tip and stencil. I repeat this process until the nail tip is the color I want.

Airbrushing Technicals

STEP 5

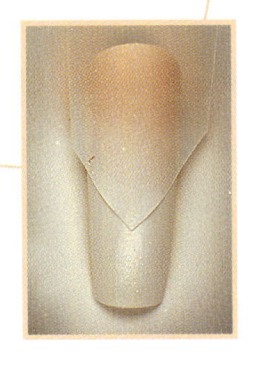

Chevron French tip application with a hand-cut nail mask: There are a number of items you may use to hand-cut the nail mask for a chevron French manicure. Anything hard that has the desired angle would be excellent to trace on the nail mask paper. (There are stencils available to trace or I use a cutting triangle which is excellent for tracing.) Using Chevron French nail masks will produce a crisp-edged white tip.

- Remove the paper backing on your mask paper. (Scrunch one end of the paper between your fingers to start separating it.) Place the nail mask paper on a piece of glass. Place the item to be traced at the top of your mask paper. Trace the chevron point onto the mask paper with the mask knife. Repeat the procedure until you have ten nail masks—one for each finger.
- Place the nail mask over each finger, protecting the nail bed color and exposing the nail tip to be sprayed. Use your finger or thumb (no nails) to press the mask tightly to the nail. If the nail mask is not tight, paint may get under it.
- Mist the nail tip white. Build the color slowly on each nail tip, to avoid getting the paint wet and runny. If the paint becomes wet, it may bleed the color under the nail mask. When airbrushing ten nails I work on five at a time to avoid overspraying the white and getting the paint wet. (Watch the edge of your nail mask. The paint easily accumulates and may run down onto the nail. Blow air to dry the nail mask and nail tip if it gets wet.) Repeat this process until the nail tip is the color desired.
- When you remove the nail masks, be sure to peel the masks back off the nail. If you pull the masks straight up off the nails, the masks may pull paint with them.

STEP 6

If the nails you are working on are very curved, you may have to touch up the stenciled nails. Using your stencil, roll the finger sideways and carefully line up the stencil with the white tip already sprayed. Mist the sides of the nail to match and complete the white tip.

STEP 7

Add a chevron-shaped lunula or moon with the remaining piece when you cut the chevron mask, or use a chevron-shaped stencil to create this unique look. Mist the lunula slightly lighter the nail tip color.

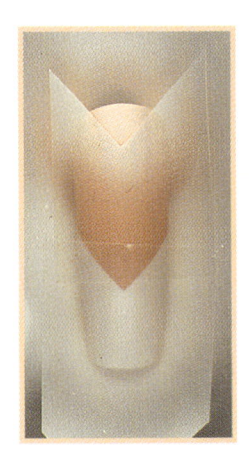

STEP 8

After you have completed all nails, apply your nail paint bonder and let it dry for three minutes. Apply the airbrush paint protective glaze for durability.

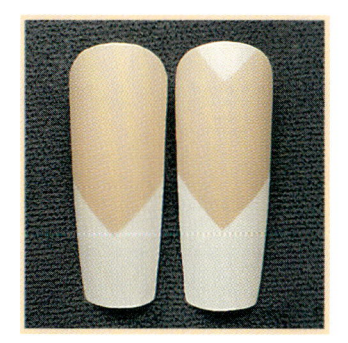

STEP 9

This photo shows the two chevron French manicure techniques next to each other. The left nail tip was done with a chevron stencil; the right nail tip was created with a hand-cut chevron nail mask, both pieces of the nail mask were used from the one cut.

Technical 7: Chevron French Manicure with Stripe

This is a simple mask trick designed to create a stripe on the nail that lasts as long as the nail color. The stripe will not peel or separate from the nail. This is an elegant choice for most conservative clients who wish to dress up their nails. It's an ideal choice for a bridal party.

Supplies

Base coat
Airbrush cleaner
Cleaning station
French manicure pink
Fuschia opal airbrush color
Shimmer or highlight (optional)
Chevron stencil or hand-cut mask
Hand-cut mask supplies:
— Uncut mask paper
— Mask knife
— Triangle
— Glass plate
Dry paper or terry towel
White nail tip color
Nail paint bonder
Protective glaze

STEP 1

Apply a clear base coat to the nail(s).

116   *Milady's Airbrushing for Nails*

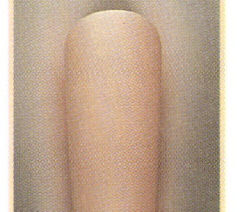

STEP 2

Choose your French manicure airbrush paint. I have chosen a French pink.

STEP 3

Optional: Add a shimmer to your French manicure paint.

STEP 4

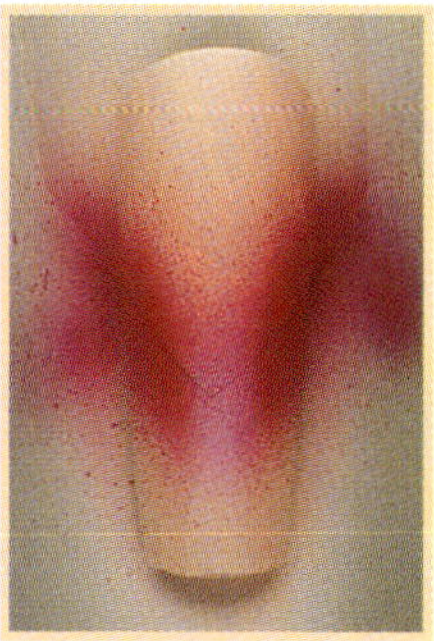

The chevron stripe and nail tip may be accomplished with a stencil or a hand-cut nail mask as previously discussed in technicals 5 and 6.

Chevron French tip application with a stencil: You will use a corner edge (90° angle) to cover the nail bed color and expose the nail tip to be sprayed. This is an excellent method for a soft-edged chevron French nail tip with a stripe.

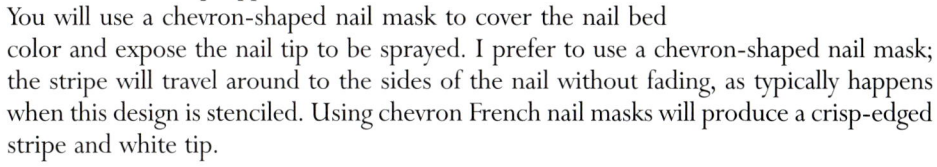

Chevron French tip application with a hand-cut nail mask: You will use a chevron-shaped nail mask to cover the nail bed color and expose the nail tip to be sprayed. I prefer to use a chevron-shaped nail mask; the stripe will travel around to the sides of the nail without fading, as typically happens when this design is stenciled. Using chevron French nail masks will produce a crisp-edged stripe and white tip.

- Place the chevron-shaped stencil or nail mask over each finger, protecting the nail bed color and exposing the nail tip to be sprayed.
- Mist the stripe color along the edge of the stencil or nail mask. It is not necessary to cover the entire nail tip, only the width of your stripe with the stripe color. I have chosen fuchsia opal as my stripe color. Build the color slowly on each nail tip, to avoid getting the paint wet and runny. If the paint becomes wet, it may bleed with the color under the stencil or nail mask. When airbrushing a set of ten nails using nail masks, I work on five nail tips at a time to avoid overspraying the paint. (Watch the edge of your stencil or nail mask. The paint accumulates easily and may run onto the nail. Blow air to dry the stencil or nail mask and nail tip if it gets wet.) Repeat this process until the stripe is the color desired.

STEP 5

If the nails are very curved, you may have to touch up the stenciling. Using your stencil, roll the finger sideways and carefully line up the stencil with the stripe color already sprayed. Mist the sides of the nail to match and complete the stripe color. This step may need to be repeated after the nail tips are stenciled with the white tip.

STEP 6

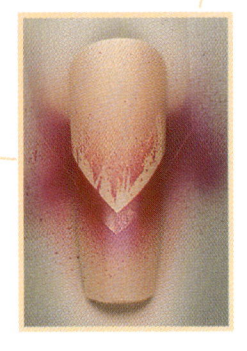

When you remove the nail masks, be sure to peel the masks back off the nail. If you pull the masks straight up off the nails, the masks may pull paint with them. Place the nail masks on a glass plate and wipe with a dry paper or terry towel to remove most of the stripe color paint. Replace the nail masks, while protecting a chevron-shaped stripe of color. If you are using a stencil, you will hold the stencil to protect a chevron-shaped stripe of color from the white tip paint.

STEP 7

Mist your white tip color onto the exposed nail tip. You will require a bit more paint to cover the overspray from dark stripes.

STEP 8

After you have completed all nails, apply your nail paint bonder and let it dry for three minutes. Apply the airbrush paint protective glaze for durability.

STEP 9

This photo shows two nail tips with striped chevron French manicures. Both designs were completed using a hand-cut chevron-shaped nail mask. The left nail tip was the nail created in our technical with a French pink nail bed color and a fuchsia opal stripe; the right nail tip is a French nude nail bed color with a pearl purple stripe.

118   Milady's Airbrushing for Nails

Technical 8: STENCIL MOVE DESIGN

The use of stencils to create designs is the most popular form of airbrushing in current use. Stencils are made from many materials. The most popular is plastic because you can see through it for your designs and it is easily cleaned after use.

I have used a plastic stencil edge to create the design below. There are many pre-cut stencils available, or you may use a mask knife to design a stencil edge of your own.

Supplies

BASE COAT
AIRBRUSH CLEANER
CLEANING STATION
STENCIL, EITHER PLASTIC OR PAPER
MASK PAPER, IF NEEDED
MASK KNIFE, IF NEEDED
FUSCHIA OPAL AIRBRUSH COLOR
OPAQUE BLACK
PEARL TURQUOISE AIRBRUSH COLOR
NAIL PAINT BONDER
PROTECTIVE GLAZE

STEP 1

Apply your base coat to the nail(s). Use a crystalline base coat for transparent airbrush nail paint or to neutralize the color of the nail plate or nail tip.

STEP 2

Mist your nail color onto the nail(s). I have chosen a fuchsia opal as my nail color. I would apply this to all ten nails.

STEP 3

Hold your stencil parallel to the nail to avoid scratching the painted surface. I place my fingers on each side of the stencil to "mold" the stencil to the curve of the nail. Mist your first design color on the stencil, at the cut-out points of the stencil edge. This will create the darkest color where the design fades into the background color. I have chosen to use black as my first design color.

STEP 4

I have pivoted the stencil up the nail tip from the first pattern sprayed and moved the edge across the center of the nail. Mist the design color at the points of the stencil edge. Pivot the stencil to the top of the nail tip (cuticle area) and create a third pattern.

STEP 5

The three stencil moves have created an interesting design. You may leave it as is or repeat steps 4 and 5 with a second color. To add additional colors to this pattern, place the stencil slightly below the first color sprayed. I have misted pearl turquoise as my second color.

STEP 6

After you have completed all nails, apply your nail paint bonder and let it dry for three minutes. Apply the airbrush paint protective glaze for durability.

STEP 7

These three nail tips display three different patterns accomplished with a stencil. The first nail tip on the left has a monochromatic color scheme. Opaque coral was the nail color with a red-orange and white stencil moved around the nail tip to create the peaks. The design was accomplished by spraying on the stencil at the peak of the stencil edge, creating a dark point that fades into the nail color. The center nail tip was the result of this technical. The nail tip on the right was accomplished spraying transparent magenta at the top of the nail and transparent violet at the bottom of the nail. Then opaque pink, pearl gold and pearl turquoise were sprayed through the stencil, moving the stencil so the pattern changed each time.

Airbrushing Technicals

Technical 9: STENCIL PICTURE

There are many stencils available today to create beautiful pictures on your client's nails. There are stencils with images of animals, tropical scenes, people, places and much more. I prefer to use plastic stencils which you can see through so it is easier to line up the images in your picture.

I have used a plastic stencil to create the stencil seaside picture below. There are many pre-cut stencils available, or you may use a mask knife to cut a stencil design of your own.

Supplies

BASE COAT
AIRBRUSH CLEANER
CLEANING STATION
PRE-CUT PLASTIC DESIGN STENCILS OF THE FOLLOWING DESIGNS:
— LIGHTHOUSE
— BOATS OF 2 DIFFERENT SIZES
— CLOUDS
— SMALL DOT
— BIRDS
MASK PAPER, IF NEEDED TO CUT OWN DESIGN
MASK KNIFE, IF NEEDED TO CUT OWN DESIGN
TRANSPARENT MAGENTA AIRBRUSH PAINT
STRAIGHT-EDGE STENCIL; PAPER OR BUSINESS CARD
OPAQUE AQUA
OPAQUE BLACK
OPAQUE WHITE
TRANSPARENT YELLOW
NAIL PAINT BONDER
PROTECTIVE GLAZE

STEP 1

Apply your base coat to the nail(s). For this design I used a crystalline base coat since I will be using transparent airbrush nail paint.

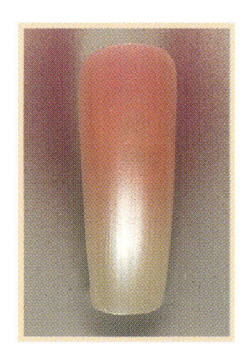

STEP 2

Airbrush transparent magenta around the cuticle area in a horseshoe shape of the nail tip. I applied more color to the top of the nail allowing the transparent magenta to fade into the crystalline base coat in the center of the nail.

STEP 3

Use a straight-edge stencil (business card or edge of paper will work) to protect the upper two-thirds of the nail, exposing the nail tip. I have chosen opaque aqua for my water.

STEP 4

Place a lighthouse stencil on the water line at one side of the nail tip. Mist opaque black to create the lighthouse in the distance.

STEP 5

Place a boat stencil in the water and mist opaque white. I have placed two sizes of boats, one larger so it appears to be in the foreground and one smaller so it appears to be in the distance.

STEP 6

To add clouds, I chose a stencil with a few different-shaped clouds. Place the top edge of the stencil against the nail with the other edge slightly elevated. Mist opaque white on the stencil at the top edge. This will create a cloud with one edge crisp and the other edge soft and faded. I added a sun in opaque white.

STEP 7

To add more detail, I placed a piece of uncut nail mask over the sails, leaving the boat part open. I placed the stencil over the white image and misted transparent yellow on the base of both boats. I used a small dot stencil to mist a yellow center in my sun. I added birds in the horizon with opaque black. I used the dull edge of my mask knife to scratch wave lines into the opaque aqua, which exposes the crystalline base coat and creates the illusion of subtle whitecaps.

STEP 8

After you have completed all nails, apply your nail paint bonder and let it dry for three minutes. Apply the airbrush paint protective glaze for durability.

STEP 9

When the client chooses to wear a picture design on only one or two nails, use two or three of the colors in the design to create a color fade on the other nails. In our seaside scene, I would have airbrushed the other nails with transparent magenta in the cuticle area, fading into the crystalline base coat, and applied the opaque aqua at the nail tip. You may also have applied the opaque white through the middle of the nail instead of leaving the crystalline base coat to show through.

STEP 10

The finished design will be a great addition to your display board. I have placed a safari scene on the right for inspiration! I used transparent colors in the background with opaque color for the animals and vegetation. Contrasting transparent with opaque paint colors creates the illusion of depth in the nail design.

Airbrushing Technicals

Technical 10:
Hand-Cut Nail Masks —Striping

Nail striping has been done for many years. Most people use striping tape or a striper brush to create the stripes accomplished in most nail art. The drawback with striping tape was that it peeled easily off the nail. The striper brush required a steady hand to apply straight stripes.

Airbrushed nail stripes are easily applied and will remain on the nail until removed. This design may be conservative or bold depending on the color schemes used.

Supplies

Glass plate
Ruler
Mask paper
Triangle, 4″ to 6″
Crystalline base coat
Tweezer
Transparent yellow
Transparent green
Transparent or pearl blue
Opaque white
Transparent red-orange
Transparent red
Transparent red-violet
Nail paint bonder
Protective glaze

STEP 1

You will need your glass plate with a ruler mounted on it (described in Chapter 6: Airbrush and Supplies). I prefer to have the centimeter edge down; it allows me to cut thinner stripes than the inches side. The ruler should be at the top of the glass plate. Remove the backing from your uncut nail mask paper. Place the mask paper along the ruler; place the center of the sheet down first and then smooth from the center out to the sides. I will use a triangle to cut my stripes. A four or six inch triangle is easy to control.

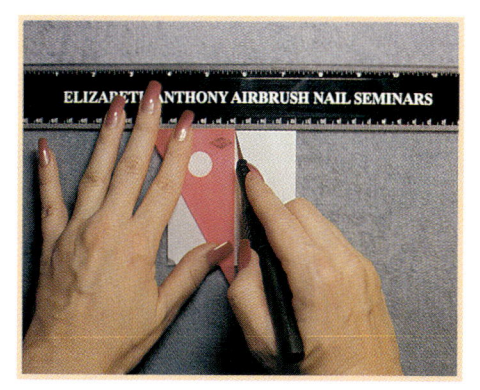

STEP 2

We are going to use the glass plate and triangle as you would a drafting board. The triangle will keep your straight edge stable to prevent any movement while cutting. Line the corner of your triangle with a line on the mounted ruler. I have chosen a stripe size of 2 mm. Hold the mask knife with your dominant hand and the triangle with the other. Move the ruler and cut every 2 mm or the size you have chosen. Check your stripes after you have cut them for any irregularities (the end pieces usually are not even and if you moved, the piece may be irregular). If you are left-handed, flip the triangle from the way you see it in the photo, so you are holding the knife in your left hand and the triangle in your right. Avoid crossing your wrists when cutting mask paper, to avoid injury.

STEP 3

If you would like a point on your stripes, as in this design, trace the angle side of your triangle over your cut stripes to develop a point. If you are going to do ten nails, you will need to cut mirror-image pointed stripes by flipping the triangle over.

STEP 4

Apply your base coat to the nail(s). For this design I used a crystalline base coat since I will be using transparent airbrush nail paint. Airbrush transparent yellow deeper at the nail tip edge fading into the crystalline base coat. Use your knife (or a tweezer) to lift a piece of nail mask from the glass plate. Place your first stripe over the transparent yellow, covering the deepest yellow at the edge where it fades into the crystalline base coat.

Airbrushing Technicals   *127*

STEP 5

Mist transparent green through the center of the nail, overlapping the transparent yellow. Place your second stripe where it catches the yellow green and a hint of the crystalline base coat at the top.

STEP 6

Mist transparent or pearl blue at the top of the nail tip, overlapping the transparent green. Place your third nail mask. I chose to have it travel straight up the nail catching all the colors including the pearl blue in its point.

STEP 7

Lightly mist the nail with opaque white. Place a few additional stripes catching the pastel colors developed by the light coating of opaque white.

STEP 8

Mist opaque white until the nail is white. I have used white as a base for the transparent paints I am going to use now. If this design appears on only a few nails, I would use the color fade on all the other nails. Apply the opaque white to all nails as a base.

STEP 9

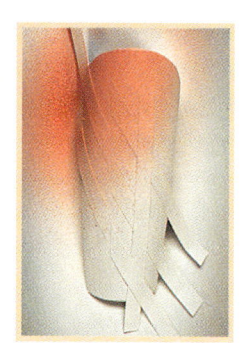

Since I have used blue at the top of the nail, I will choose a complementary color for a bold contrast. I have chosen transparent red-orange which is in the triad of orange, the color opposite blue on the color wheel. This will contrast with the blue in the stripe. Mist all the nails with the transparent red-orange.

STEP 10

To contrast the green stripe, I have chosen transparent red as the color for the center of the nail. Mist the red so it slightly overlaps the red-orange.

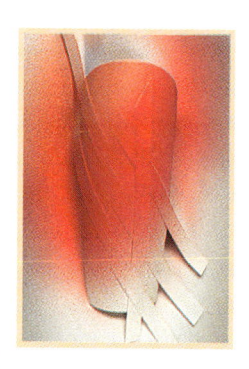

STEP 11

To contrast the yellow stripe, I will choose red-violet as my final color. Mist transparent red-violet at the nail tip, slightly overlapping the red. You now have the triad of red as the color-fade applied on all nails.

STEP 12

Remove your nail masks with a pair of tweezers or your fingers. You must peel the nail masks straight back, similar to the motion used to peel a banana. If you pull up on the masks, they may create suction and lift the paint. Remove the nail masks in the opposite order you placed them down.

Airbrushing Technicals

STEP 13

After you have completed all nails, apply your nail paint bonder and let it dry for three minutes. Apply the airbrush paint protective glaze for durability.

STEP 14

The completed stripe designs are striking on every nail or on one or two with the color fade on the remaining nails. The nail tip on the left was created using transparent magenta and violet over a crystalline base coat. I used thicker stripes to cover the colors. I used opaque white and then pearl gold as my color fade, using the gold at each edge of the nail and letting the white remain through the middle. Gold is opposite violet on the color wheel (gold is the "metal" color for yellow) and is an excellent contrast for magenta and violet.

The center nail tip is the finished design we completed in the step-by-step above. The final nail tip was accomplished by misting transparent yellow and dark green, placing nail mask stripes of different widths. Mist opaque white lightly and place a few more nail mask stripes to cover the pastel greens that developed. Cover the nail with pearl gold and mist the corners with opaque or pearl red. All three of the nail designs used the complementary contrast color schemes and contrasted the transparent paint with the opaque paint to create the illusion of depth and movement within the design.

Technical 11:

Pre-cut Nail Masks: Positive and Negative Use

To save time and to have a number of nail masks of the same shape, investigate pre-cut nail masks. These nail masks are cut on a press and new designs are slowly becoming available. The pre-cut nail masks are attached to a paper backing with an inside piece, called the negative, and an outside piece, called a positive. A negative mask protects an area that is already painted, preventing that area from changing. Nothing is happening under the mask, so it is a negative area.

The opposite is true of the positive mask. This mask protects the surroundings of the design and exposes an area that will change. Something is happening in the area that the mask exposes, so it is a positive area. You may use either term inside piece or negative mask. It is important to understand this terminology when you are exposed to other airbrush technicals or advanced texts.

Supplies

Base coat
Airbrush cleaner
Cleaning station
Transparent magenta
Pre-cut masks, both negative and positive
Transparent violet
Opaque white
Opaque black
Nail paint bonder
Protective glaze

STEP 1

Apply your base coat to the nail(s).

Airbrushing Technicals — 131

STEP 2

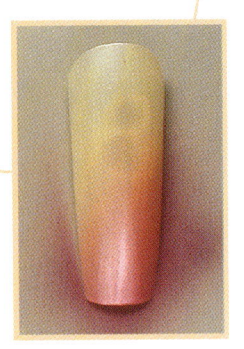

Mist transparent magenta at the lower outer corner of the nail(s).

STEP 3

Remove the first negative mask from the paper backing. The easiest way to remove the nail mask is to squish the nail mask paper between your index finger and thumb. This will cause the nail mask to rumple and the mask film will easily separate from the paper backing. Place the nail mask on the nail, covering the deepest magenta at the edge fading into the crystalline base coat.

STEP 4

Mist transparent violet through the center and at the top of the nail tip, so it overlaps the transparent magenta. Place your second mask as shown in the photo, covering the violet and crystalline base coat at the top.

STEP 5

Mist opaque white until the nail appears white. If the design is on only one nail, mist the other nails opaque white to match the designed nail.

132   Milady's Airbrushing for Nails

STEP 6

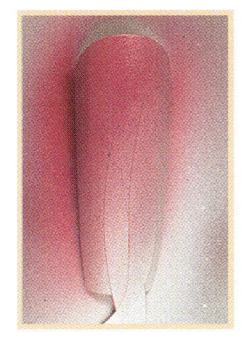

Mist transparent magenta at the top of the nail at a diagonal, fading into the opaque white. I am going to leave the lower half of the nail white. Notice how bright the transparent magenta is over opaque white. Mist the other nails to match.

STEP 7

Remove the positive mask from the paper backing. Place the positive mask opening next to the negative already on the nail. I have placed the positive mask to mist a shadow behind the design I have already masked off. To figure out how to place the shadow, determine your light source. Since the lower half of the nail is lighter, the light is coming from below and off to the right on this nail tip. It will be the opposite on the other hand. I have lightly misted opaque black so you can see the outline of the positive mask next to the negative mask.

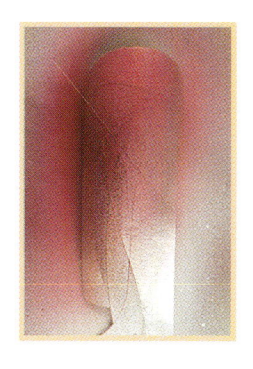

STEP 8

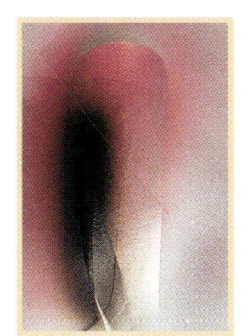

Be sure there is no other exposed nail other than the shape in the positive mask. If the nail is exposed, cut a piece of mask paper to cover the opening to prevent the black from getting on the nail. Mist the opaque black until it is a solid color.

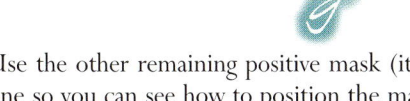

STEP 9

Use the other remaining positive mask (it is easier to use a clean one so you can see how to position the mask) and place it next to the other negative mask. Mist opaque black. Remove the positive masks and you will have two shadows.

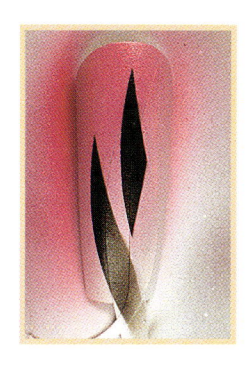

Airbrushing Technicals   *133*

STEP 10

Remove the negative nail masks. After you have completed all nails, apply your nail paint bonder and let it dry for three minutes. Apply the airbrush paint protective glaze for durability.

STEP 11

If this design is applied to nails on opposite hands, remember to create a mirror image of the design on the other hand.

STEP 12

When practicing these technicals, I recommend practicing them precisely the way I have outlined. Then experiment with different color schemes. In this photo, I have sprayed this design with three different color schemes. The nail tip on the left is done in a monochromatic color scheme. I have used different hues of red-violet (magenta). The center nail tip is the triad of red-violet, using red-violet and violet in the design. The nail tip on the right is an example of using the complementary contrast for your design. I have contrasted red-violet with yellow and green. By varying the color scheme, one design may be customized for a number of people.

Technical 12: Pre-cut Mask Design with Stenciled Background

There are many combinations of design tools that you can make. I enjoy combining stencils and nail masks to create unique designs. In this technical, I will use design masks first and then stencils to create a patterned background.

Supplies

BASE COAT
AIRBRUSH CLEANER
CLEANING STATION
TRANSPARENT YELLOW-ORANGE
NEGATIVE WHEAT-SHAPED PRE-CUT MASK OR HAND-CUT MASK
TRANSPARENT RED-ORANGE
PEARL ELECTRIC BLUE
OPAQUE WHITE
OPAQUE CORAL
TRANSPARENT RED-ORANGE
NAIL PAINT BONDER
PROTECTIVE GLAZE

STEP 1

Apply your base coat to the nail(s).

STEP 2

Mist transparent yellow-orange at the base of the nail tip on the diagonal, darker at the nail tip fading into the crystalline base coat. Place the negative mask across the yellow-orange nail tip up into the crystalline white. I am using a wheat-shaped pre-cut mask, the ribbon end.

STEP 3

Mist transparent red-orange through the middle third of the nail, overlapping the yellow-orange. Place the second negative wheat mask through the different colors developed.

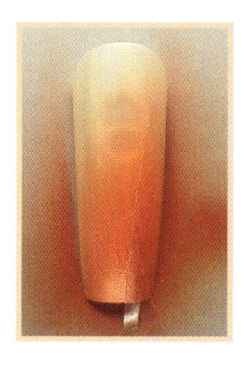

STEP 4

Mist pearl electric blue at the top half of the nail. Place the third negative wheat mask through the pearl electric blue.

STEP 5

Mist opaque white over the entire nail. It will take more white at the top of the nail to cover the dark blue. I find it easier to apply this design on more than one nail. You can apply one coat of white to each nail and then repeat the process until the nail appears white. You are less likely to overspray and get the paint wet.

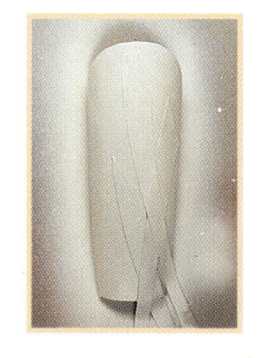

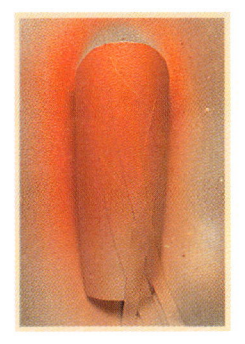

STEP 6

Mist the nail with opaque coral. If you are going to put color on all the other nails and only design a few, apply the opaque coral to all the nails. Then apply transparent red-orange to the top half of the nail(s) for the color fade.

STEP 7

Place your stencil over the nail and mist pearl blue through it. I moved the stencil to repeat the pattern around the nail.

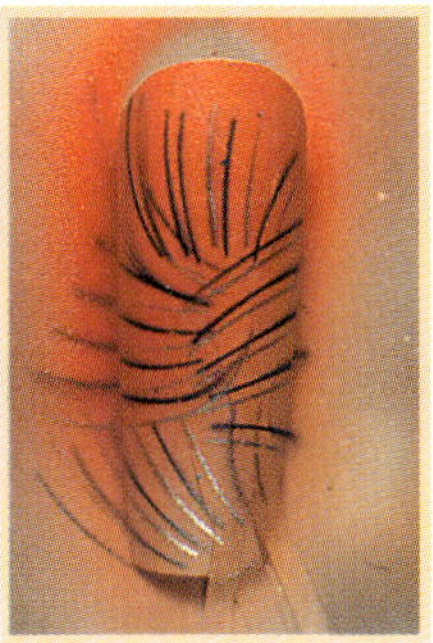

STEP 8

Repeat the stencil pattern slightly off to one side of the previous one with pearl white.

STEP 9

Carefully remove the nail masks, reversing the order they were applied. After you have completed all nails, apply your nail paint bonder and let it dry for three minutes. Apply the airbrush paint protective glaze for durability.

Airbrushing Technicals

STEP 10

This combination of nail mask and stencil creates many fascinating looks. The first nail tip on the left uses the negative wheat mask (the other end) and saves transparent yellow, red and violet. Pearl pink is used for the background color; two different stencil patterns are used in pearl silver and pearl turquoise. The center nail is the nail accomplished by this technical. The last nail tip on the right is accomplished with the negative flame mask and transparent yellow, magenta and violet. The background color is pearl gold with two stencil patterns applied over it in black and pearl purple.

Technical 13:

Stencil Pattern with Pre-cut Mask Design

Another method of combining the use of stencil and nail masks is employed in this design. I will stencil a pattern and then use transparent paints to create colors. I will place nail masks with each color to create another design over the stenciled pattern.

Supplies

Base coat
Airbrush cleaner
Cleaning station
Stencil: fabric called webbing
Negative flame masks
Transparent magenta
Transparent burgundy
Transparent violet
Pink opal shimmer
Opaque black
Nail paint bonder
Protective glaze

STEP 1

Apply your base coat to the nail(s).

STEP 2

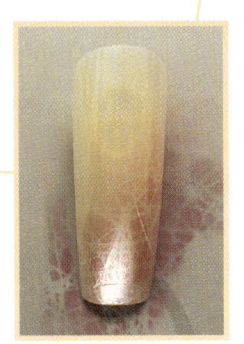

Hold a stencil over the nail. I am using a plastic fabric called "webbing" for my pattern. Place the fabric over the nail and mist transparent magenta through it. Place the negative flame mask over the patterned nail tip.

STEP 3

Mist transparent burgundy through the webbing stencil over the middle third of the nail, overlapping the transparent magenta. Place the second negative flame mask.

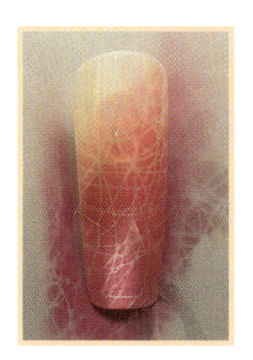

STEP 4

Mist transparent violet through the webbing stencil over the top third of the nail, overlapping the transparent burgundy. Place the third negative flame mask.

STEP 5

Mist opaque black lightly (so you can still see the webbing pattern) over the exposed nail tip. To add sheen I have misted a pink opal shimmer over the black.

STEP 6

Carefully remove the nail masks in reverse order of application.

STEP 7

After you have completed all nails, apply your nail paint bonder and let it dry for three minutes. Apply the airbrush paint protective glaze for durability.

STEP 8

There are many stencil patterns to choose from for this design. The first nail on the left has a star stencil pattern with transparent magenta, yellow and yellow-green for overlay colors. A negative lightning bolt mask was applied with each color. White was lightly misted to define the lightning bolts. The middle nail is the completed design from this technical. The last nail on the right is a zebra pattern stencil with transparent burgundy and violet. White was lightly misted to outline the design; a lilac opal shimmer was applied for sheen.

You can have a lot of fun using transparent paints to "color" in your stenciled pattern. Experiment with unique combinations of your design tools and see what you can create!!

Technical 14: Using a Stencil as a Design Template

There are several ways to use pre-cut stencils. You can place the stencil on the nail and spray color through it to see the design. I like to use the stencil as a design template. I frequently find that when I use a stencil directly on a nail, I scratch the nail color underneath or get a fuzzy edge on my design. So I tend to use this technique to create custom-cut nail masks for my customers. I cut the designs during slow times in the day or while watching TV at home. The designs are saved and ready to use on glass plates stored in my roll-about.

Supplies

Base coat
Airbrush cleaner
Cleaning station
Positive hand-cut or pre-cut stencil of flower and pistil
Uncut nail mask paper
Glass plate
#11 mask knife
Opaque white
Pearl pink
Positive hand-cut mask or pre-cut stencil of leaf design
Pearl green
Transparent yellow
Transparent blue
Transparent violet
Nail paint bonder
Protective glaze

STEP 1

Place the stencil over uncut nail mask paper that has been applied to a glass plate. (I have lightly sprayed the nail mask white so it is visible on top of the glass plate.) I will use this two-piece flower stencil as my design template.

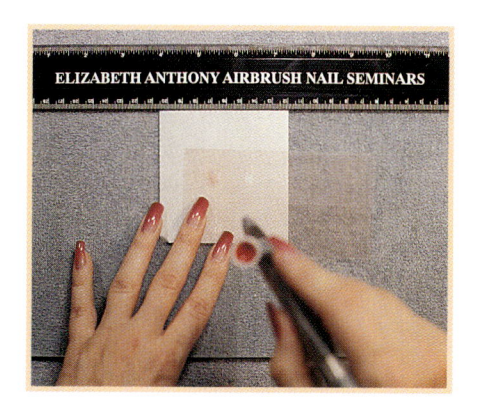

STEP 2

Hold the stencil in place over the uncut nail mask paper. Lightly and slowly mist paint through the stencil so the image is outlined on your mask paper. Do not remove stencil until paint is dry to avoid smearing.

STEP 3

When the stencil is removed, we have a perfect image of the two-piece stencil on the nail mask paper.

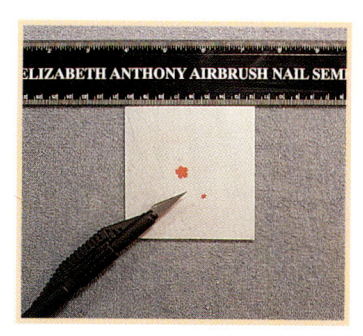

STEP 4

Using a sharp #11 mask knife, trace the outline of the flower and the pistil. You will end up with a mask that you can use like a stencil (called a positive mask since the area that is exposed is the area that is changing) and the two inside pieces which you cut out. The two little pieces are considered negative masks since nothing happens in the area that they cover. Save these pieces for another design. Be creative!

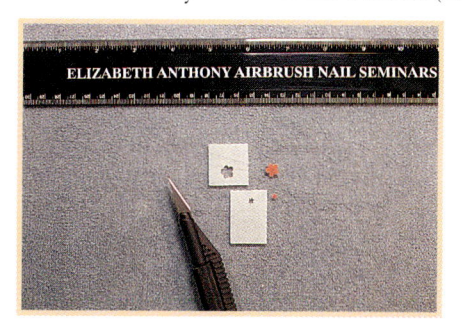

Airbrushing Technicals

STEP 5

Apply your base coat to the nail or nail tip in this case. I will be working with opaque color so a clear base coat is fine.

STEP 6

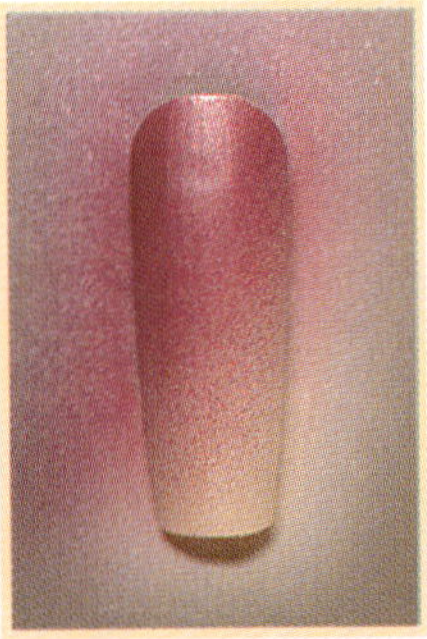

I have chosen a subtle color fade using white and a pink pearl for this design. Apply this color fade to all the other nails, even if they are not going to have any nail art applied. Always airbrush all the nails (and the toenails if they let you!).

STEP 7

Using a leaf design cut from mask paper, I have placed the design on the nail and sprayed opaque white to block the colors underneath from showing through.

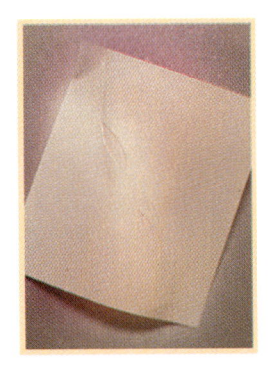

STEP 8

Mist pearl green through the positive nail mask for the leaf color. To give the leaf more depth, spray transparent yellow at the top of the leaf and transparent blue at the bottom.

144 *Milady's Airbrushing for Nails*

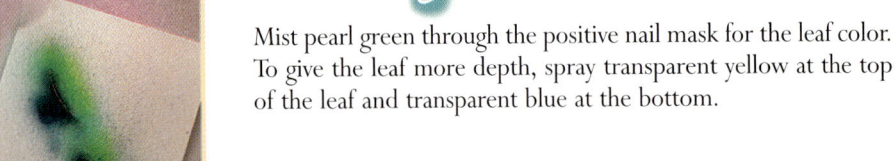

STEP 9

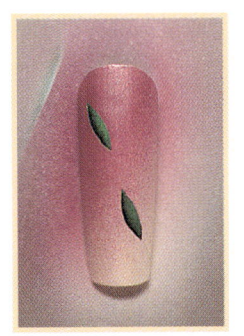

This tri-toning of the leaves will give the leaves more definition. The transparent colors change the pearl green to a light green on top, a pearl green through the middle and a dark pearl green at the bottom.

STEP 10

Place the large flower nail mask centered between the leaves. Be sure to cover any exposed nail tip with uncut nail mask paper. Block out with opaque white. Then mist violet lightly around the edges of the nail mask. I actually spray on the positive nail mask edge allowing the airbrush color overspray to tint the edges of the flower.

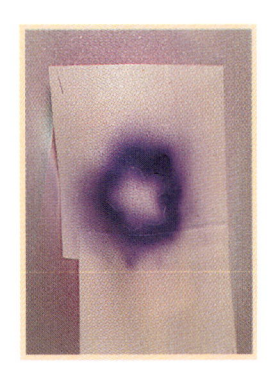

STEP 11

The flower petals will have graduated color. The flower petals are the lightest in the center, deepening in color as they go out to the edge of the petal.

STEP 12

Place the second nail mask for the pistils in the center of the flower. Spray opaque white and then yellow.

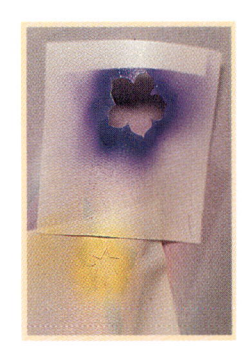

Airbrushing Technicals   145

STEP 13

Remove the nail mask to expose a feminine flower. I have used the dull side of my nail mask knife to scratch detail into the center of the flower. Apply airbrush paint bonder and airbrush nail glaze.

STEP 14

This photo shows a few additional nail tips using the same technique of cutting custom nail masks by using a pre-cut stencil as a template. There are so many stencils available to stimulate your imagination. When first cutting your own images in nail mask paper, try stencil designs with as few curves as possible. Straight lines are the easiest to trace. With practice the curves will become easier. When tracing a curve, try rolling the mask knife in your fingers to follow the image's curves. You will find the images you trace on mask paper will not always match the stencil perfectly, but that is what makes it a custom design!

STEP 15

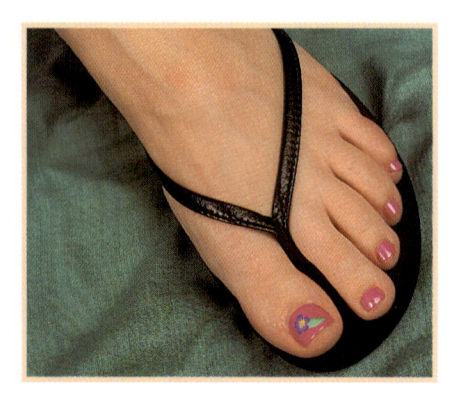

This technique is excellent for toenails, too. Many conservative women will not wear nail art on their fingernails but will love it on their toes. Their toenails are hidden in shoes while they are at work, but they may display them at home to feel special.

146   Milady's Airbrushing for Nails

Glossary

Absorbs—the ability of dark colors to take in all visible light waves and heat from that light.
Actuator—a lever located on underside of an American-manufactured New Technology double-action airbrush that needs to be set to + to make sure plunger pin inside the airbrush is out of the way prior to insertion of the nozzle.
Adjuster lever—same as actuator.
Aerosol nail paints—inexpensive paints for use with design stencils and tools.
Air tank regulator—also called control valve; regulates release of air from compressed air tanks into airbrush hoses.
Air hose couplings—threaded part of airhose that attaches to compressor and airbrush.
Air pressure regulator—used to set air pressure on most compressors.
Airbrush nail color display board—a board used to showcase the colors of airbrush nail color.
Airbrush paint cleaner—a product for cleaning airbrush paint.
Ash—a color produced when black paint mixes with an opaque color that contains white paint.
Automatic shut-off—a feature on a compressor that prevents operation until the trigger of the airbrush is depressed.
Automatic thermal protection—feature that shuts off a compressor when in danger of overheating.

Base coat—the first coat applied to nails prior to application of airbrushed nail paint.
Basic colors—the primary colors of red, yellow and blue.
Blanking plug—a small black plug placed in opening opposite placement of the color cup on the American-manufactured New Technology double-action airbrush.
Bottle-mix method—technique to create new nail colors by mixing the colors in a bottle.
Braided rubber hose—a rubber hose with a braided fabric cover recommended for use with traditional metal airbrushes.
Bumpering—applying polish to the entire nail, the nail sides and nail tip to seal the nail inside the polish.

Cancel—the effect of combining opposite colors on the wheel.
Chroma—color

Cleaning station—jars and rags to spray the airbrush into during cleaning.
Coiled plastic hose—type of airbrush hose that stretches when in use and recoils when not in use.
Color blends or color fades—when two or more airbrush paints are misted overlapping each other on the nail.
Color-match—producing nail color paints to match fabrics or traditional nail polishes.
Color scheme—overall mood conveyed by color choice.
Complimentary contrast—a color combination found on opposite sides of the wheel that produces the highest intensity of color, such as red and green.
Compressed air tank—an air source contained in a cylinder, usually available at a beverage supply or welding company.
Compressed gas cylinder—see compressed air tank.
Compressor regulator—adjusts the pressure on a compressor.
Condensing—when droplets of water cool and collect.
Cool colors—green to blue-violet on the color wheel.
Crystalline base coat—a special effect polish with small crystals that reflect light.

Design tool—used to create images on nails such as pictures, letters or graphics.
Disconnects—specialty fittings that eliminate threaded fittings, which are attached to airbrush and hose.
Diaphragm or small piston compressor—smallest and most economical air compressor available.

Emulsion—the liquid in which the paint pigment is suspended.
External bleeder valve—a part of the air compressor that must be open prior to turning compressor on. The bleeder valve is reduced to emit a small amount of air when compressor starts.

Fluid nozzle—part of the airbrush where the needle is inserted. Also called tip. Nozzle releases paint when needle is retracted.
Foam board—board made of foam and posterboard; used to practice spraying or displaying nail tips, also called foamcore.
Foundation color—nail color chosen by client that is used at the start.
French manicures—nail color application that uses a soft tone on nail bed with a white nail tip.
Frisket paper—clear tacky paper with a paper backing that can be used to cut nail designs.

Glass prism—glass or crystal that reflects the colors in light.
Gravity feed—an airbrush in which gravity pulls the paint into the airbrush.
Gray—a color produced when a black paint mixes with white paint.

Head assemblies—the front section of the airbrush; usually consists of the needle cap, nozzle cap, and possibly the fluid nozzle.

Hue—another word for color.

In-line moisture traps—a cylinder placed in the airbrush hose to collect moisture.

Interference colors—metallic finishes or special effects that produce a gold shimmer or opalescent shimmer reflected by light.

Intermediate colors—combination of one primary color and one secondary color. Also called tertiary colors.

Internal mix—blending of paint with air inside the airbrush.

Knob—same as needle adjusting screw.

Manifolds—hardware that allows you to attach more than one airbrush and air hose to a single compressor or gas cylinder regulator.

Medium—the liquid in which the paint pigment is suspended.

Mirror-image—designs on the right hand should be reflections of the designs on the left hand.

Moisture separator—attachment to the end of the airbrush hose that helps reduce water buildup in the hose.

Mono—one

Monochromatic—one color.

MSDS Sheets—Material Safety Data Sheets, supplied by the manufacturers of nail products.

Multi-manifold—also called multiple outlet hose adapter; hardware that allows you to connect four or more airbrush hoses to a single compressor or gas cylinder regulator.

Muted—a less intense color produced by adding the complimentary contrast of a color.

Nail paint bonder—a nail product that wets the dried airbrush nail paint and seals it to the base coat; increases nail color durability.

Nail mask paper—clear tacky paper with a paper backing that can be used to cut nail designs.

Needle adjusting screw—a knob on the airbrush that controls the paint spray.

Needle—part of airbrush that is drawn back for the airbrush to release paint.

Needle chuck—the end screw on the airbrush that is loosened to clean or replace the needle.

Negative mask—inside piece of a pre-cut nail mask.

No load—air compressors without airbrushes or hoses attached.

Oil-less compressor—use air instead of oil to cool the motor.

Opalescent—type of base coat or paint with reflective qualities.

Opaque—colors that are not see-through; generally produced by adding white, black or gray to pure colors.
OSHA—Occupational Safety and Hazards Administration.
Overspray—spray that goes off the nail into the air or onto a surface.
Paint color change—changing of colors during an airbrush service.
Paint formula—a record detailing how many drops of each paint color was required to achieve the new color.
Pearlescent—frosted nail color
Pigment—the chemical in paint that creates the color we see.
Positive mask—outside piece of a pre-cut nail mask.
Pounds per square inch (psi)—measurement of the amount of air fed into airbrush hose by an air source.
Power cleaning—a technique that involves squirting the cleaner directly into the airbrush while simultaneously pulling back on the trigger and blowing out the airbrush cleaner.
Practice nail tips—plastic tips that simulate real nails.
Pre-cut nail mask—pre-prepared designs made of mask paper to design nails.
Pressure adjusting knob—used to adjust air pressure and to lock in desired pressure on pressure regulator for air source.
Pressure gauge—tells the amount of air released from an air tank regulator or compressor; the pressure gauge is located on the pressure regulator.
Primary colors—the basic colors of yellow, blue and red.
Propellant can adapter valve—regulates amount of air released into air hose.
Protective nail glaze—a thick glaze for use after the paint bonder dries that helps prevent wear off the edges of the nail.
Pure colors—a transparent primary, secondary, or intermediate color on the perimeter or edge of a traditional color wheel.
Quick connects—specialty fittings that eliminate threaded fittings, which are attached to air brush and hose.
Reamer—a tool that looks like a needle with a sharp point which will scrap paint from the inside of the nozzle.
Reflects—the ability of colors to bounce off a surface.
Reservoir—hole in the top of the airbrush where drops of paint are placed. Also called a well.
Seated—positioning of the needle fitted into the fluid nozzle to prevent paint release until the trigger is pulled back.
Secondary colors—colors produced by mixing two primary colors producing orange, green and violet.
Shade—gradation of darker values.

Shimmer—type of base coat with reflective qualities.
Small color cup—container located on top or side of airbrush for paint to be placed in the airbrush.
Solid nail color—one color covering the entire nail.
Special effect base coat—type of base coat that enhances the airbrushed nail color.
Spray-mix method—technique used to create a new nail color by spraying first one color paint and then overlapping another color.
Stencil—the most common design tool; made of plastic, paper or fabric, with images cut into it.
Storage and silent compressor—larger and more expensive type of air compressor.
Straight plastic hose—type of airbrush hose made of plastic.
Striper brush—tool for creating stripes.
Striping tape—adhesive lines for creating stripes.
T-manifold—hardware that allows you to connect two airbrush hoses to a single compressor or gas cylinder regulator.
Teflon tape—also known as plumber's tape; used around the tank outlet of a compressed air tank to prevent air seepage.
Tertiary colors—combination of one primary color and one secondary color. Also called intermediate colors.
Thin topcoat—a nail product that helps adhere the airbrush nail paint to the base coat.
Tint—gradation of lighter values.
Tip—see fluid nozzle
Traditional nail polish—nail lacquer applied with brush supplied in bottle; hand-applied nail color.
Transition—in terms of color, it's a new color created by two overlapping transparent colors.
Transparent—colors that are see-through.
Tri—three
Tri-manifold—also called cross-junction; hardware that allows you to connect three airbrush hoses to a single compressor or gas cylinder regulator.
Triad of a color—the true color and the section of color next to it on either side.
Under load—air compressors with airbrushes and hoses attached.
Value—lightness or darkness of a color.
Warm colors—red through yellow colors on the color wheel.
Well—opening on top of airbrush for paint to be placed into the airbrush.

Index

A

Acetone, 16, 20, 21, 22, 76
Acrylic paints, 41, 80
Actuators (adjuster levers), 12, 13, 84
Adapters, 37–38
Adjustable wrenches, 16
Adjusting knobs, 35–36
Adjusting screws, 5, 8, 10
Aerosol paints, 42
African-American clients, 70
Air canisters, 27–28
Air compressors, 31–35
   hoses for, 26, 36, 37
   manifolds for, 38
   troubleshooting for, 83, 84
Air filters, 35
Air hose couplings, 37
Air hose manifolds, 29, 36, 38–39
Air hoses, 26
   compressed air tanks and, 30
   diaphragm compressors and, 32
   moisture separators and, 36–37
   pressure regulators and, 35
   propellant air canisters and, 28
Air pressure gauges, 29
Air pressure regulators, 29, 31, 35–36, 83
Air sources, 26–39
Air tank regulators, 29, 31, 35–36, 83
Air tanks, 27, 28–31
Airbrush apparatuses, 3–25, 77–85
Ammonia, 43
Artificial nails, 43, 45–46
Ash effect, 63, 64

Automatic shut-off feature, 33, 84
Automatic thermal protection, 32–33, 34

B

Base coats, 43–44, 45–46, 74, 104. *See also* Crystalline base coats
Base colors. *See* Pure colors
Basic colors. *See* Primary colors
Beverage supply companies, 28
Black paint, 53, 54, 55, 62, 63
Blanking plugs, 13, 14
Bleeder valves, 33–34
Bonders. *See* Thin topcoats
Bottle-mix method, 66
Braided rubber hoses, 26
Brain, 68
Bridal parties, 92
Built-in bleeder valves, 34
Bumpering, 44, 45, 46, 74, 75

C

Cancelled colors, 65
Canisters, 27–28
Carbon dioxide tanks, 28, 29, 31, 83
Chevron French manicures, 88, 92, 112–118
Christmas, 59
Cleaning routines, 19–23, 25
Cleaning supplies, 15–16, 24. *See also* Paint cleaner
Clear nail polish, 75
Coiled plastic hoses, 26
Color analysis, 69

153

Color contour, 99–100
Color cups, 4
   cleaning of, 16, 22, 24
   of double-action airbrushes, 9, 12, 13, 14, 15
   empty, 77
   of single-action airbrushes, 6–7
   See also Paint color change
Color fades, 90, 101–106
Color matching, 67, 91–92
Color schemes, 57–62
Color theory, 50–70
Color value, 54
Color wheel, 51–53, 54–57
Complementary contrast, 57, 58–59, 60, 64, 65
Compressed air tanks, 27, 28–31
Compressor regulators, 32, 38
Condensation, 36
Contrasting colors, 57
Control valves, 29, 31, 35–36, 83
Cool colors, 51, 68–69
Cross-junctions, 38–39
Crystalline base coats, 44
   on artificial nails, 45
   multiple color fades over, 104
   stencil move designs over, 119
   stencil pictures over, 123, 124
   striping over, 127
   transparent/opaque color over, 53, 54

D

Daily equipment cleaning, 19–23, 25
Dental facilities, 68
Design tools, 42, 46–48. *See also* Mask paper; Stencils
Designs, 69–70, 90
Diaphragm compressors, 27, 28, 31–32
Discount salons, 89
Displays, 48–49, 61–62, 88, 92
Distilled water, 54, 80, 84
Double-action airbrushes. *See* New technology double-action airbrushes; Traditional double-action airbrushes

Drain valves, 36, 83
Dull colors, 64

E

Electrical supply, 31, 34, 35, 84
Emulsions, 62
End-of-the-day equipment cleaning, 19–23, 25
External bleeder valves, 33–34

F

Fabric matching, 67, 91–92
Filters, 35
"First free time" deals, 88, 89, 90
Fluid nozzles, 3
   cleaning of, 20, 22–23, 24–25, 77–79
   damaged, 81
   improper attachment of, 79
   incorrect size of, 80
   of new technology double-action air brushes, 12, 13, 14–15, 24–25, 84
   of single-action airbrushes, 6, 7–8, 20, 78–79
   of traditional double-action airbrushes, 9, 11, 22–23, 78–79
   See also Nozzle caps
Fluorescent lighting, 51
Foam board (foamcore), 48
Foundation colors, 58
Freehand work, 46
French manicures
   aerosol paints and, 42
   Chevron type, 88, 92, 112–118
   clear base coats for, 45, 108
   dark skin and, 70
   marketing of, 88
   muted colors for, 65
   technique for, 107–118
   time required for, 87, 90
Frisket paper. *See* Mask paper
Frosted (pearlescent) paints, 41, 65–66, 102, 106

G

Give-aways, 88, 89, 90
Glass prisms, 50–51
Glazes, 44–46, 75, 92
Gold shimmer paints, 66
Gravity-feed feature, 4
Gray effect, 63, 64
Grease (lubricants), 16, 19, 82–83

H

Hair industry, 86–87, 89
Hand-cut nail masks, 88
    for Chevron French manicures, 114, 115, 117, 118
    for French manicures, 109
    for striping, 126–130
    See also Pre-cut nail masks
HCS (Hazard Communication Standard) Files, 41
Head assemblies
    bubbling cleaner around, 82
    daily cleaning of, 20, 21–23
    improper attachment of, 79
    spattering problems and, 81
Hoses. *See* Air hoses
Hue. *See* Color…
Human brain, 68

I

In-line moisture traps, 37
Incandescent lighting, 51
Industrial diaphragm compressors, 32
Initials, 48
Inside pieces. *See* Negative masks
Interference colors. *See* Special effect paints
Interior decoration, 68
Intermediate (tertiary) colors, 52, 53, 59
Internal bleeder valves, 34
Internal mix feature, 4
Irritated skin, 43

K

Knobs (needle adjusting screws), 5, 8, 10

L

Lighting, 51
Lubricants, 16, 19, 82–83. *See also* Oil

M

Maintenance
    moisture separators, 36
    new technology double-action airbrushes, 23–25
    storage compressors, 35
    traditional double-action airbrushes, 19, 23
Manifolds, 29, 36, 38–39
Manufacturer's liability, 43. *See also* MSDS Sheets
Marketing, 86–93
Mask paper, 46, 47
    for design templates, 143, 145, 146
    for stencil pictures, 124
    See also Hand-cut nail masks; Pre-cut nail masks
Mechanical problems, 77–85
Medical facilities, 68
Medium (emulsion), 62
Metallic finishes. *See* Special effect paints
Mirror-image designs, 48
Mixed colors, 62
Moisture separators, 26, 35, 36–37, 83
Monochromatic schemes, 57, 58
MSDS Sheets, 41
Multi-action rollers, 14
Multi-manifolds, 39
Multiple color fades, 104–106
Muted colors, 65

N

Nail bumpering, 44, 45, 46, 74, 75
Nail color. *See* Color…
Nail designs. *See* Designs
Nail glazes, 44–46, 75, 92
Nail mask paper. *See* Mask paper
Nail paint. *See* Paint…

Index   *155*

Nail polish. *See* Traditional nail polish
Nail polish remover, 76
Nail tips. *See* Plastic nail tips
Needle adjusting screws, 5, 8, 10
Needle caps, 16, 20, 22
Needle chucks, 5, 18, 80
Needles, 3–4
    cleaning of, 16
    damaged, 81–82
    lubrication of, 19
    removal of, 18, 20
    replacement of, 21, 23
    stuck, 82
    tightening of, 80
Negative masks, 47, 48, 131–134, 143
New technology double-action airbrushes, 3
    cleaning of, 16, 18, 25
    maintenance of, 23–25
    troubleshooting for, 78, 79, 80, 81–82, 83, 84
    types of, 12–15
Newton, Isaac, 50
Noise, 31–32
Nozzle caps, 20
Nozzles. *See* Fluid nozzles

O

O-rings, 19, 82
Oil, 35. *See also* Lubricants
Opalescent paints, 41, 44, 45, 66
Opaque colors, 53, 54, 62, 64
OSHA (Occupational Safety and Hazards Administration), 41

P

Paint bonders. *See* Thin topcoats
Paint bottles, 42, 80. *See also* Color cups
Paint cleaner, 43
    bubbling of, 82
    dilution of, 71
    for nozzle cleaning, 78
    on stuck needles, 82

Paint color. *See* Color...
Paint color change, 15, 16, 18, 24
Paint formulas, 62
Paint supplies, 40–49, 80
Paintbrushes
    for color cup cleaning, 15, 24
    for design work, 48
    for nozzle cleaning, 24
    residue removal with, 18
Pearlescent paints, 41, 65–66, 102, 106
Periodic maintenance. *See* Maintenance
Pictures, 122–125
Pigments, 54. *See also* Color...
Pipe cleaners, 16, 21
Plastic fabric, 140
Plastic hoses, 26, 36, 37
Plastic nail tips
    display of, 48–49, 61–62, 88, 92
    practice on, 48, 71, 72–73
Plastic stencils, 119, 122
Plastic washers, 29, 30
Positive masks, 48, 131–134, 143
"Power cleaning," 24, 25
Practice techniques, 71–73
Pre-cut nail masks, 46, 47–48
    positive/negative use of, 131–134
    stenciled background with, 135–138
    stenciled pattern with, 139–141
    See also Hand-cut nail masks
Pressure adjusting knobs, 35–36
Pressure gauges, 29
Pressure regulators, 29, 31, 35–36, 83
Price lists, 89–90
Primary colors
    defined, 52
    mixing of, 55, 56, 64
    naming of, 53
Prisms, 50–51
Propellant air canisters, 27–28
Protective nail glazes, 44–46, 75, 92
Pure colors, 51
    on color wheel, 54–55, 56, 57
    in design, 61
    in triads, 58

Q
Quick connects/disconnects, 37

R
Reamers, 25
Referrals, 91
Regulators
    air pressure, 29, 31, 35–36, 83
    compressor, 32, 38
Reservoirs. *See* Color cups
Rollers, 14
Rubber hoses, 26

S
St. Patrick's Day, 69
Sanders, Robert, 86
Sealers, 44–46, 75, 92
Seasonal skin categories, 69
Secondary colors, 52, 53
Shades, 54, 56, 59, 63
Shimmer paints, 44, 45, 65–66
Shut-off valves, 37. *See also* Automatic shut-off feature
Silent compressors, 27, 34–35
Single-action airbrushes, 3
    cleaning supplies for, 16
    daily cleaning of, 19–21
    troubleshooting for, 78, 79, 80, 82
    types of, 5–8
Skin cleansing, 75
Skin color, 69, 70
Skin irritation, 43
Small piston compressors, 27, 28, 31–32
Solid nail color, 97–98
Special effect paints, 44, 45, 66. *See also* Pearlescent paints
Spray-mix method, 66
Spray regulators, 16, 20, 22
Stencil move designs, 119–121
Stencil pictures, 122–125
Stencils, 46, 47
    aerosol paints and, 42
    for backgrounds, 135–138
    for Chevron French manicures, 113, 115, 117
    as design templates, 142–146
    for French manicures, 108–109
    pre-cut mask designs and, 139–141
    time for, 90
Storage compressors, 27, 34–35
Straight plastic hoses, 26
Striping, 116–118, 126–130
Styluses, 48

T
T-manifold/junctions, 38, 39
Technical problems, 77–85
Technical procedures, 97–146. *See also* Practice techniques
Tertiary (intermediate) colors, 52, 53, 59
Thermal protection, 32–33, 34
Thin topcoats, 44, 75
    application problems with, 85
    on artificial nails, 45
    client-owned, 45, 46
Tints
    on color wheel, 56
    complementary contrast of, 59
    defined, 54
    mixing of, 63
    in triads, 58
Tips (fluid nozzles). *See* Fluid nozzles
Toenail airbrushing, 75, 88, 111, 146
Traditional double-action airbrushes, 3
    daily cleaning of, 21–23
    hoses for, 26
    maintenance of, 19, 23
    needle removal from, 18–19
    troubleshooting for, 78, 79, 80, 81, 82, 83
    types of, 8–12
Traditional French manicures. *See* French manicures
Traditional nail polish
    abandonment of, 88
    color matching with, 67–68, 92
    durability of, 75

revenue generated by, 86, 89–90
skin proximity to, 69
time required for, 87, 90
See also Nail polish remover
Transitional colors, 62, 64, 102, 103
Transparent colors, 53, 54, 62. *See also* Clear nail polish
Tri-manifolds, 38–39
Triad of a color, 57, 58, 59, 60
Triggers
    of double-action airbrushes, 8–9, 10–11, 14, 19, 21, 23
    malfunctioning of, 82–83
    of single-action airbrushes, 8, 21
Troubleshooting, 77–85
True colors. *See* Pure colors
Two-color fades, 101–103

U

U.S. Occupational Safety and Hazards Administration, 41

V

Value (color), 54
Valves
    bleeder, 33–34
    control, 29, 31, 35–36, 83
    drain, 36, 83
    shut-off, 37. *See also* Automatic shut-off feature

W

Warm colors, 51, 68–69
Warranties, 33
Washers, 29, 30
Water condensation, 36
Webbing, 140
Welding supply companies, 28
Wells. *See* Color cups
White paint, 53, 54, 62, 63
Window cleaner, 43
Winter holidays, 59, 66, 88
Wrenches, 16